MAKE MON
BUILD WI

MAKE MONEY AND BUILD WEALTH

A Goldmine of Advice by
Napoleon Hill, Wallace D Wattles,
PT Barnum and Franklyn Hobbs

Compiled by Abhishek Rana

Vitasta

Published by
Renu Kaul Verma
Vitasta Publishing Pvt Ltd
4348/4C, Ansari Road, Daryaganj
New Delhi - 110 002
info@vitastapublishing.com

ISBN: 978-81-19670-86-4
© Vitasta TIMELESS CLASSICS
First Edition 2024
MRP ₹295

Compiled by Abhishek Rana
Typeset & Cover Design by Rohit Gautam
Printed by Vikas Computer and Printers, New Delhi

Contents

THE ART OF MONEY GETTING
by PT Barnum

THE SECRET OF WEALTH
by Franklyn Hobbs

ARTICLES ON MAKING MONEY

To all those who aspire
to become rich.

Introduction

It is a universal fact that money is necessary for our survival. Money sustains our livelihood and makes it possible for us to lead a comfortable and safe life. To be able to live on one's own terms and have all the suitable luxury is every person's dream but only few people are able to achieve that.

What, then, should be done to put oneself on the path of wealth?

This question has occupied some of the greatest thinkers across the globe. This volume of Make money and Build Wealth brings words of wisdom from esteemed personalities like Benjamin Franklin, one of the founding fathers of the USA, Theodore Roosevelt, the 26th president of the USA, the bestselling authors Napoleon Hill, and Wallace D Wattles and showman and businessman PT Barnum, to illuminate the minds of readers of all ages who suffer from uncertainty and lack of confidence when it comes to taking the next step toward the path of prosperity.

SECTION ONE

THINK AND GROW RICH
by Napoleon Hill

'You are the master of your destiny. You can influence,
direct and control your own environment. You can make
your life what you want it to be.'

Desire

The Starting Point of all Achievement

When Edwin C Barnes climbed down from the freight train in Orange, New Jersey, more than thirty years ago, he may have resembled a tramp, but his thoughts were those of a king!

As he made his way from the railroad tracks to Thomas A Edison's office, his mind was at work. He saw himself standing in Edison's presence. He heard himself asking Mr Edison for an opportunity to carry out the one consuming obsession of his life, a burning desire to become the business associate of the great inventor.

Barnes' desire was not a hope! It was not a wish! It was a keen, pulsating desire, which transcended everything else. It was definite.

The desire was not new when he approached Edison. It had been Barnes' dominating desire for a long time. In the beginning, when the desire first appeared in his mind, it may have been, probably was, only a wish, but it was no mere wish when he appeared before Edison with it.

A few years later, Edwin C Barnes again stood before Edison, in the same office where he first met the inventor. This time his desire had been translated into reality. *He was in business with Edison.* The dominating dream of his life had become a reality. Today, people who know Barnes envy him, because of the 'break' life yielded him. They see him in the days of his triumph, without taking the trouble to investigate the *cause* of his success.

Barnes succeeded because he chose a definite goal, placed all his energy, all his will power, all his effort, everything back to that goal. He did not become the partner of Edison the day he arrived. He was content to start in the most menial work, as long as it provided an opportunity to take even one step towards his cherished goal.

Five years passed before the chance he had been seeking made its appearance. During all those years not one ray of hope, not one promise of attainment of his desire had been held out to him. To everyone, except himself, he appeared only another cog in the Edison business wheel, but in his own mind, he was the partner of Edison, every minute of the time, from the very day that he first went to work there.

It is a remarkable illustration of the power, of a definite desire, Barnes won his goal, because he wanted to be a business associate of Mr Edison, more than he wanted anything else. He created a plan by which to attain that purpose. But he burned all bridges behind him. He stood by his desire until it became the dominating obsession of his life–and–finally, a fact.

When he went to Orange, he did not say to himself, 'I will try to induce Edison to give me a job of some sort.' He said, 'I will see Edison, and put him on notice that I have come to go into business with him.'

He did not say, 'I will work there for a few months, and if I get no encouragement, I will quit and get a job somewhere else.' He did say, 'I will start anywhere. I will do anything Edison tells me to do, but *before I am through*, I will be his associate.'

He did not say, 'I will keep my eyes open for another opportunity, in case I fail to get what I want in the Edison organisation.' He said, 'There is but one thing in this world that I am determined to have, and that is a business association with Thomas A Edison. I will burn all bridges behind me, and stake my entire future on my ability to get what I want.'

He left himself no possible way of retreat. He had to win or perish!

That is all there is to the Barnes story of success!

A LONG WHILE ago, a great warrior faced a situation which made it necessary for him to make a decision which insured his success on the battlefield. He was about to send his armies against a powerful foe, whose men outnumbered his own. He loaded his soldiers into boats, sailed to the enemy's country, unloaded soldiers and equipment, then gave the order to burn the ships that had carried them. Addressing his men before the first battle, he said, 'You see the boats going up in smoke. That means that we cannot leave these shores alive unless we win! We now have no choice—*we win or we perish!*' They won.

Every person who wins in any undertaking must be willing to burn his ships and cut all sources of retreat. Only by so doing can one be sure of maintaining that state of mind known as a burning desire to win, essential to success.

THE MORNING AFTER the great Chicago fire, a group of merchants stood on State Street, looking at the smoking remains of what had been their stores. They went into a conference to decide if they would try to rebuild, or leave Chicago and start over in a more promising section of the country. They reached a decision--all except one–to leave Chicago.

The merchant who decided to stay and rebuild pointed a finger at the remains of his store, and said, 'Gentlemen, on that very spot I will build the world's greatest store, no matter how many times it may burn down.'

That was more than fifty years ago. The store was built. It stands there today, a towering monument to the power of that state of mind known as a burning desire. The easy thing for Marshal Field to have done, would have been exactly what his fellow merchants did. When the going was hard, and the future looked dismal, they pulled up and went where the going seemed easier.

Mark well this difference between Marshal Field and the other merchants, because it is the same difference which distinguishes Edwin C Barnes from thousands of other young men who have worked at the Edison organisation. It is the same difference which distinguishes practically all who succeed from those who fail.

Every human being who reaches the age of understanding of the purpose of money, wishes for it. *Wishing* will not bring riches. But *desiring* riches with a state of mind that becomes an obsession, then planning definite ways and means to acquire riches, and backing those plans with persistence which *does not recognise failure*, will bring riches.

The method by which desire for riches can be transmuted

into its financial equivalent, consists of six practical steps:

1. Fix in your mind the *exact* amount of money you desire. It is not sufficient merely to say 'I want plenty of money.' Be definite as to the amount. (There is a psychological reason for definiteness which will be described in a subsequent chapter).

2. Determine exactly what you intend to give in return for the money you desire. (There is no such reality as 'something for nothing'.)

3. Establish a definite date when you intend to *possess* the money you desire.

4. Create a definite plan for carrying out your desire, and begin *at once*, whether you are ready or not, to put this plan into *action*.

5. Write out a clear, concise statement of the amount of money you intend to acquire, name the time limit for its acquisition, state what you intend to give in return for the money, and describe clearly the plan through which you intend to accumulate it.

6. Read your written statement aloud, twice daily, once just before retiring at night, and once after arising in the morning. As you read--see and feel and believe yourself already in the possession of money.

It is important that you follow the instructions described in these six steps. It is especially important that you observe, and follow the instructions in the sixth paragraph. You may complain that it is impossible for you to 'see yourself in possession of money' before you actually have it. Here is where a burning desire will come to your aid. If you truly desire money so keenly that your desire is an obsession, you will have no difficulty in convincing yourself that you will acquire it.

The object is to want money, and to become so determined to have it that you convince yourself you will have it.

Only those who become 'money conscious' ever accumulate great riches. 'Money consciousness' means that the mind has become so thoroughly saturated with the desire for money, that one can see one's self already in possession of it.

To the uninitiated, who has not been schooled in the working principles of the human mind, these instructions may appear impractical. It may be helpful, to all who fail to recognise the soundness of the six steps, to know that the information they convey, was received from Andrew Carnegie, who began as an ordinary labourer in the steel mills, but managed, despite his humble beginning, to make these principles yield him a fortune of considerably more than one hundred million dollars.

It may be of further help to know that the six steps here recommended were carefully scrutinised by the late Thomas A Edison, who placed his stamp of approval upon them as being, not only the steps essential for the accumulation of money, but necessary for the attainment of *any definite goal*.

The steps call for no 'hard labour.' They call for no sacrifice. They do not require one to become ridiculous, or credulous. To apply them calls for no great amount of education. But the successful application of these six steps does call for sufficient *imagination* to enable one to see, and to understand, that accumulation of money cannot be left to chance, good fortune, and luck. One must realise that all who have accumulated great fortunes, first did a certain amount of dreaming, hoping, wishing, desiring, and planning *before* they acquired money.

You may as well know, right here, that you can never have riches in great quantities, unless you can work yourself into a white heat of desire for money, and actually believe you will possess it.

You may as well know, also that every great leader, from the dawn of civilisation down to the present, was a dreamer.

If you do not see great riches in your imagination, you will never see them in your bank balance.

Never, in the history of America has there been so great an opportunity for practical dreamers as now exists. The six-year economic collapse has reduced all men, substantially, to the same level. A new race is about to be run. The stakes represent huge fortunes which will be accumulated within the next ten years. The rules of the race have changed, because we now live in a changed world that definitely favours the masses, those who had but little or no opportunity to win under the conditions existing during the depression, when fear paralysed growth and development.

We who are in this race for riches, should be encouraged to know that this changed world in which we live is demanding new ideas, new ways of doing things, new leaders, new inventions, new methods of teaching, new methods of marketing, new books, new literature, new features for the radio, new ideas for moving pictures. Back of all this demand for new and better things, there is one quality which one must possess to win, and that is definiteness of purpose, the knowledge of what one wants, and a burning desire to possess it.

The business depression marked the death of one age, and the birth of another. This changed world requires practical dreamers who can, *and will* put their dreams into action. The practical dreamers have always been, and always will be the pattern-makers of civilisation.

We who desire to accumulate riches, should remember the real leaders of the world always have been men who harnessed, and put into practical use, the intangible, unseen forces of unborn opportunity, and have converted those forces, (or impulses of thought), into sky-scrapers, cities, factories, airplanes, automobiles, and every form of convenience that makes life more pleasant.

Tolerance, and an open mind are practical necessities of the dreamer of today. Those who are afraid of new ideas are doomed before they start. Never has there been a time more favourable to pioneers than the present. True, there is no wild and woolly west to be conquered, as in the days of the Covered Wagon; but there is a vast business, financial, and industrial world to be remoulded and redirected along new and better lines.

In planning to acquire your share of the riches, let no one influence you to scorn the dreamer. To win the big stakes in this changed world, you must catch the spirit of the great pioneers of the past, whose dreams have given to civilisation all that it has of value, the spirit which serves as the life-blood of our own country--your opportunity and mine, to develop and market our talents.

Let us not forget, Columbus dreamed of an Unknown world, staked his life on the existence of such a world, and discovered it!

Faith

Visualisation of Desire

Faith is the head chemist of the mind. When faith is blended with the vibration of thought, the subconscious mind instantly picks up the vibration, translates it into its spiritual equivalent, and transmits it to Infinite Intelligence, as in the case of prayer.

The emotions of faith, love, and sex are the most powerful of all the major positive emotions. When the three are blended, they have the effect of 'colouring' the vibration of thought in such a way that it instantly reaches the subconscious mind, where it is changed into its spiritual equivalent, the only form that induces a response from Infinite Intelligence.

Love and faith are psychic; related to the spiritual side of man. Sex is purely biological, and related only to the physical. The mixing, or blending, of these three emotions has the effect of opening a direct line of communication between the finite, thinking mind of man, and Infinite Intelligence.

How to Develop Faith?

There comes, now, a statement which will give a better understanding of the importance the principle of auto-suggestion assumes in the transmutation of desire into its physical, or monetary equivalent; namely: Faith is a state of mind which may be induced, or created, by affirmation or repeated instructions to the subconscious mind, through the principle of auto-suggestion.

As an illustration, consider the purpose for which you are, presumably, reading this book. The object is, naturally, to acquire the ability to transmute the intangible thought impulse of desire into its physical counterpart, money. By following the instructions laid down in the chapters on auto-suggestion, and the subconscious mind, as summarised in the chapter on auto-suggestion, you may convince the subconscious mind that you believe you will receive that for which you ask, and it will act upon that belief, which your subconscious mind passes back to you in the form of 'Faith,' followed by definite plans for procuring that which you desire.

The method by which one develops faith, where it does not already exist, is extremely difficult to describe, almost as difficult, in fact, as it would be to describe the colour of red to a blind man who has never seen any colour, and has nothing with which to compare what you describe to him. Faith is a state of mind which you may develop at will, after you have mastered the thirteen principles, because it is a state of mind which develops voluntarily, through application and use of these principles.

Perhaps the meaning may be made clearer through the

following explanation as to the way men sometimes become criminals. Stated in the words of a famous criminologist, 'When men first come into contact with crime, they abhor it. If they remain in contact with crime for a time, they become accustomed to it, and endure it. If they remain in contact with it long enough, they finally embrace it, and become influenced by it.'

This is the equivalent of saying that any impulse of thought which is repeatedly passed on to the subconscious mind is, finally, accepted and acted upon by the subconscious mind, which proceeds to translate that impulse into its physical equivalent, by the most practical procedure available.

In connection with this, consider again the statement, all thoughts which have been emotionalised, (given feeling) and mixed with faith, begin immediately to translate themselves into their physical equivalent or counterpart.

The emotions, or the 'feeling' portion of thoughts, are the factors which give thoughts vitality, life, and action. The emotions of Faith, Love, and Sex, when mixed with any thought impulse, give it greater action than any of these emotions can do singly.

Not only thought impulses which have been mixed with faith, but those which have been mixed with any of the positive emotions, or any of the negative emotions, may reach, and influence the subconscious mind.

From this statement, you will understand that the subconscious mind will translate into hits physical equivalent, a thought impulse of a negative or destructive nature, just as readily as it will act upon thought impulses of a positive or constructive nature. This accounts for the strange phenomenon which so many millions of people experience, referred to as 'misfortune,' or 'bad luck.'

There are millions of people who believe themselves 'doomed' to poverty and failure, because of some strange force over which they believe they have no control. They are the creators of their own 'misfortunes,' because of this negative believe, which is picked up by the subconscious mind, and translated into its physical equivalent.

This is an appropriate place at which to suggest again that you may benefit, by passing on to your subconscious mind, any desire which you wish translated into its physical, or monetary equivalent, in a state of expectancy or belief that the transmutation will actually take place. Your belief, or faith, is the element which determines the action of your subconscious mind. There is nothing to hinder you from 'deceiving' your subconscious mind when giving it instructions through autosuggestion, as I deceived my son's subconscious mind.

To make this 'deceit' more realistic, conduct yourself just as you would, if you were already in the possession of the material which you are demanding, when you call upon your subconscious mind.

The subconscious mind will transmute into its physical equivalent, by the most direct and practical media available, any order which is given to it in a state of belief, or faith that the order will be carried out.

Surely, enough has been stated to give a starting point from which one may, through experiment and practice, acquire the ability to mix faith with any order given to the subconscious mind. Perfection will come through practice. It *cannot* come by merely *reading* instructions.

If it be true that one may become a criminal by association with crime, (and this is a known fact), it is equally true that one may develop faith by voluntarily suggesting to the subconscious mind that one has faith. The mind comes, finally, to take on the nature of the influences which dominate it. Understand this truth, and you will know why it is essential for you to encourage the *positive emotions* as dominating forces of your mind, and discourage--and *eliminate* negative emotions.

A mind dominated by positive emotions, becomes a favourable abode for the state of mind known as faith. A mind so dominated may, at will, give the subconscious mind instructions, which it will accept and act upon immediately.

Faith is a state of mind which can be induced by the power of auto-suggestion.

All down the ages, the religionists have admonished struggling humanity to 'have faith' in this, that, and the other dogma or creed, but they have failed to tell people HOW to have faith. They have not stated that 'faith is a state of mind, and that it may be induced by self-suggestion.'

In language which any normal human being can understand, we will describe all that is known about the principle through which faith may be developed, where it does not already exist.

Have Faith in yourself; Faith in the infinite. Before we begin, you should be reminded again that:

Faith is the '*eternal elixir*' which gives life, power, and action to the impulse of thought!

The foregoing sentence is worth reading a second time, and a third, and a fourth. It is worth reading aloud!

Faith is the starting point of all accumulation of riches!

Faith is the basis of all '*miracles*,' and all mysteries which cannot be analysed by the rules of science!

Faith is the only known antidote for failure!

Faith is the element, the '*chemical*' which, when mixed with prayer, gives one direct communication with Infinite Intelligence.

Faith is the element which transforms the ordinary vibration of thought, created by the finite mind of man, into the spiritual equivalent.

Faith is the only agency through which the cosmic force of Infinite Intelligence can be harnessed and used by man.

Every one of the foregoing statements are capable of proof!

The proof is simple and easily demonstrated. It is wrapped up in the principle of autosuggestion. Let us centre our attention, therefore, upon the subject of self-suggestion, and find out what it is, and what it is capable of achieving.

It is a well-known fact that one comes, finally, to believe whatever one repeats to one's self, *whether the statement be true or false*. If a man repeats a lie over and over, he will eventually accept the lie as truth. Moreover, he will believe it to be the truth. Every man is what he is, because of the dominating thoughts which he permits to occupy his mind. Thoughts which a man deliberately places in his own mind, and encourages with sympathy, and with which he mixes any one or more of the emotions, constitute the motivating forces, which direct and control his every movement, act, and deed!

Comes, now, a very significant statement of truth:

Thoughts which are mixed with any of the feelings of emotions, constitute of 'Magnetic' force which attracts, from the vibrations of the ether, other similar, or related thoughts. A thought thus 'magnetised' with emotion may be compared to a seed which, when planted in fertile soil, germinates, grows, and multiplies itself over and over again, until that which was originally one small seed, becomes countless millions of seeds of the same brand!

The ether is a great cosmic mass of eternal forces of vibration. It is made up of both destructive vibrations and constructive vibrations. It carries, at all times, vibrations of fear, poverty, disease, failure, misery; and vibrations of prosperity, health, success, and happiness, just as surely as it carries the sound of hundreds of orchestrations of music, and hundreds of human voices, all of which maintain their own individuality, and means of identification, through the medium of radio.

From the great storehouse of the ether, the human mind is constantly attracting vibrations which harmonise with that which dominates the human mind. Any thought, idea, plan, or purpose which one *holds* in one's mind attracts, from the vibrations of the ether, a host of its relatives, adds these 'relatives' to its own force, and grows until it becomes the dominating, motivating master of the individual in whose mind it has been housed.

Now, let us go back to the starting point, and become informed as to how the original seed of an idea, plan, or purpose may be planted in the mind. The information is easily conveyed: any idea, plan, or purpose may be placed in the mind *through repetition of thought*. This is why you are asked to write out a statement of your major purpose, or Definite Chief Aim, commit it to memory, and repeat it, in audible words, day after day, until these vibrations of sound have reached your subconscious mind.

We are what we are, because of the vibrations of thought which we pick up and register, through the stimuli of our daily environment.

Resolve to throw off the influences of any unfortunate environment, and to build your own life to order. Taking inventory of mental assets and liabilities, you will discover that your greatest weakness is lack of self-confidence. This handicap can be surmounted, and timidity translated into courage, through the aid of the principle of auto-suggestion. The application of this principle may be made through a simple arrangement of positive thought impulses stated in writing, memorised, and repeated, until they become a part of the working equipment of the subconscious faculty of your mind.

Auto-suggestion

There are no limitations to the mind except those we acknowledge. Both poverty and riches are the offspring of thought.

The medium for influencing the subconscious mind.

Auto-suggestion is a term which applies to all suggestions and all self-administered stimuli which reach one's mind through the five senses. Stated in another way, auto-suggestion is self-suggestion. It is the agency of communication between that part of the mind where conscious thought takes place, and that which serves as the seat of action for the subconscious mind.

Through the dominating thoughts which one *permits* to remain in the conscious mind, (whether these thoughts be negative or positive, is immaterial), the principle of auto-suggestion voluntarily reaches the subconscious mind and influences it with these thoughts.

No thought, whether it be negative or positive, can enter the subconscious mind without the aid of the principle of auto-suggestion, with the exception of thoughts picked up from the ether. Stated differently, all sense impressions which are perceived through the five senses, are stopped by the conscious thinking mind, and may be either passed on to the subconscious mind, or rejected, at will. The conscious faculty serves, therefore, as an outer-guard to the approach of the subconscious.

Nature has so built man that he has absolute control over the material which reaches his subconscious mind, through his five senses, although this is not meant to be construed as a statement that man always exercises this control. In the great majority of instances, he does not exercise it, which explains why so many people go through life in poverty.

Recall what has been said about the subconscious mind resembling a fertile garden spot, in which weeds will grow in abundance, if the seeds of more desirable crops are not sown therein. Autosuggestion is the agency of control through which an individual may voluntarily feed his subconscious mind on thoughts of a creative nature, or, by neglect, permit thoughts of a destructive nature to find their way into this rich garden of the mind.

You were instructed, in the last of the six steps described in the chapter on Desire, to read aloud twice daily the written statement of your desire for money, and to see and feel yourself already in possession of the money! By following these instructions, you communicate the object of your desire directly to your subconscious mind in a spirit of absolute faith. Through repetition of this procedure, you voluntarily create thought habits which are favourable to your efforts to transmute desire into its monetary equivalent.

Go back to these six steps described earlier, and read them again, very carefully, before you proceed further. Then (when you come to it), read very carefully the four instructions for the organisation of your 'Master Mind' group, described in the chapter on Organised Planning. By comparing these two sets of instructions with that which has been stated on auto-suggestion, you, of course, will see that the instructions involve the application of the principle of auto-suggestion.

Remember, therefore, when reading aloud the statement of your desire (through which you are endeavouring to develop a 'money consciousness'), that the mere reading of the words is of no consequence--unless you mix emotion, or feeling with your words. If you repeat the famous Emil Coué formula, 'Day by day, in every way, I am getting better and better,' without mixing emotion and faith with your words, you will experience no desirable results. Your subconscious mind recognises and acts upon only thoughts which have been well-mixed with emotion or feeling.

This is a fact of such importance as to warrant repetition in practically every chapter, because the lack of understanding of this is the main reason the majority of people who try to apply the principle of auto-suggestion get no desirable results.

Plain, unemotional words do not influence the subconscious mind. You will get no appreciable results until you learn to reach your subconscious mind with thoughts, or spoken words which have been well emotionalised with belief.

Do not become discouraged, if you cannot control and direct your emotions the first time you try to do so. Remember, there is no such possibility as something for nothing. Ability to reach, and influence your subconscious mind has its price, and you must pay that price. You cannot cheat, even if you desire to do so. The price of ability to influence your subconscious mind is everlasting persistence in applying the principles described here. You cannot develop the desired ability for a lower price. You, and you alone, must decide whether or not the reward for which you are striving (the 'money consciousness'), is worth the price you must pay for it in effort.

Wisdom and 'cleverness' alone, will not attract and retain money except in a few very rare instances, where the law of averages favours the attraction of money through these sources. The method of attracting money described here, does not depend upon the law of averages. Moreover, the method plays no favourites. It will work for one person as effectively as it will for another. Where failure is experienced, it is the individual, *not the method*, which has failed. If you try and fail, make another effort, and still another, until you succeed.

Your ability to use the principle of auto-suggestion will depend, very largely, upon your capacity to concentrate upon a given desire until that desire becomes a burning obsession.

When you begin to carry out the instructions in connection with the six steps described in the second chapter, it will be necessary for you to make use of the principle of concentration.

Let us here offer suggestions for the effective use of concentration. When you begin to carry out the first of the six steps, which instructs you to 'fix in your own mind the exact amount of money you desire,' hold your thoughts on that amount of money by concentration, or fixation of attention, with your eyes closed, until you can actually see the physical appearance of the money. Do this at least once each day. As you go through these exercises, follow the instructions given in the chapter on faith, and see yourself actually in possession of money!

Here is a most significant fact—the subconscious mind takes any orders given it in a spirit of absolute faith, and acts upon those orders, although the orders often have to be presented over and over again, through repetition, before they are interpreted by the subconscious mind. Following the preceding statement, consider the possibility of playing a perfectly legitimate 'trick' on your subconscious mind, by making it believe, *because you believe it*, that you must have the amount of money you are visualising, that this money is already awaiting your claim, that the subconscious mind must hand over to your practical plans for acquiring the money which is yours.

Hand over the thought suggested in the preceding

paragraph to your imagination, and see what your imagination can, or will do, to create practical plans for the accumulation of money through transmutation of your desire.

Do not wait for a definite plan, through which you intend to exchange services or merchandise in return for the money you are visualising, but begin at once to see yourself in possession of the money, demanding and expecting meanwhile, that your subconscious mind will hand over the plan, or plans you need. Be on the alert for these plans, and when they appear, put them into action immediately. When the plans appear, they will probably 'flash' into your mind through the sixth sense, in the form of an 'inspiration.' This inspiration may be considered a direct 'telegram,' or message from Infinite Intelligence. Treat it with respect, and act upon it as soon as you receive it. Failure to do this will be fatal to your success.

In the fourth of the six steps, you were instructed to 'Create a definite plan for carrying out your desire, and begin at once to put this plan into action.' You should follow this instruction in the manner described in the preceding paragraph. Do not trust to your 'reason' when creating your plan for accumulating money through the transmutation of desire. Your reason is faulty. Moreover, your reasoning faculty may be lazy, and, if you depend entirely upon it to serve you, it may disappoint you.

When visualising the money, you intend to accumulate, (with closed eyes), *see yourself rendering the service, or delivering the merchandise you intend to give in return for this money. This is important!*

Summary of Instructions

The fact that you are reading this book is an indication that you earnestly seek knowledge. It is also an indication that you are a student of this subject. If you are only a student, there is a chance that you may learn much that you did not know, but you will learn only by assuming an attitude of humility. If you choose to follow some of the instructions but neglect, or refuse to follow others--*you will fail!*

To get satisfactory results, you must follow all instructions in a spirit of faith.

The instructions given in connection with the six steps earlier will now be summarised, and blended with the principles covered by this chapter, as follows:

First. Go into some quiet spot (preferably in bed at night) where you will not be disturbed or interrupted, close your eyes, and repeat aloud, (so you may hear your own words) the written statement of the amount of money you intend to accumulate, the time limit for its accumulation, and a description of the service or merchandise you intend to give in return for the money. As you carry out these instructions, see yourself already in possession of the money.

For example: – Suppose that you intend to accumulate $50,000 by the first of January, five years hence, that you intend to give personal services in return for the money, in the capacity of a salesman. Your written statement of your purpose should be similar to the following:

'By the first day of January, 19.., I will have in my possession $50,000, which will come to me in various amounts from time to time during the interim.

'In return for this money I will give the most efficient service of which I am capable, rendering the fullest possible quantity, and the best possible quality of service in the capacity of salesman of (describe the service or merchandise you intend to sell).

'I believe that I will have this money in my possession. My faith is so strong that I can now see this money before my eyes. I can touch it with my hands. It is now awaiting transfer to me at the time, and in the proportion that I deliver the service I intend to render in return for it. I am awaiting a plan by which to accumulate this money, and I will follow that plan, when it is received.'

Second. Repeat this programme night and morning until you can see, (in your imagination) the money you intend to accumulate.

Third. Place a written copy of your statement where you can see it night and morning, and read it just before retiring, and upon arising until it has been memorized.

Remember, as you carry out these instructions, that you are applying the principle of auto-suggestion, for the purpose of giving orders to your subconscious mind. Remember, also, that your subconscious mind will act only upon instructions which are emotionalised, and handed over to it with 'feeling.' Faith is the strongest, and most productive of the emotions. Follow the instructions given in the chapter on faith.

These instructions may, at first, seem abstract.

Do not let this disturb you. Follow the instructions, no matter how abstract or impractical they may, at first, appear to be. The time will soon come, if you do as you have been instructed, *in spirit as well as in act*, when a whole new universe of power will unfold to you.

Scepticism, in connection with ALL new ideas, is characteristic of all human beings. But if you follow the instructions outlined, your scepticism will soon be replaced by belief, and this, in turn, will soon become crystallised into absolute faith. Then you will have arrived at the point where you may truly say, 'I am the master of my fate, I am the captain of my soul!'

Many philosophers have made the statement, that man is the master of his own *earthly* destiny, but most of them have failed to say *why* he is the master. The reason that man may be the master of his own earthly status, and especially his financial status, is thoroughly explained in this chapter.

Man may become the master of himself, and of his environment, because he has the power to influence his own subconscious mind, and through it, gain the cooperation of Infinite Intelligence.

You are now reading the chapter which represents the keystone to the arch of this philosophy. The instructions contained in this chapter must be understood and applied with persistence, if you succeed in transmuting desire into money.

The actual performance of transmuting desire into money involves the use of auto-suggestion as an agency by which one may reach, and influence, the subconscious mind.

The other principles are simply tools with which to apply auto-suggestion. Keep this thought in mind, and you will, at all times, be conscious of the important part: the principle of auto-suggestion is to play in your efforts to accumulate money through the methods described in this book.

Carry out these instructions as though you were a small child. Inject into your efforts something of the faith of a child. The author has been most careful, to see that no impractical instructions were included, because of his sincere desire to be helpful.

After you have read the entire book, come back to this chapter, and follow in spirit, and in action, this instruction:

Read the entire chapter aloud once every night, until you become thoroughly convinced that the principle of auto-suggestion is sound, that it will accomplish for you all that has been claimed for it. As you read, underscore with a pencil every sentence which impresses you favourably.

Follow the foregoing instruction to the letter, and it will open the way for a complete understanding, and mastery of the principles of success.

Imagination

The Workshop of the Mind

The imagination is literally the workshop wherein are fashioned all plans created by man. The impulse, the desire, is given shape, form, and action through the aid of the imaginative faculty of the mind.

It has been said that man can create anything which he can imagine.

Of all the ages of civilisation, this is the most favourable for the development of the imagination, because it is an age of rapid change. On every hand one may contact stimuli which develop the imagination.

Through the aid of his imaginative faculty, man has discovered, and harnessed, more of Nature's forces during the past fifty years than during the entire history of the human race, previous to that time. He has conquered the air so completely, that the birds are a poor match for him in flying. He has harnessed the ether, and made it serve as a means of instantaneous communication with any part of the world. He has analysed, and weighed the sun at a distance of millions of miles, and has determined, through the aid of imagination, the elements of which it consists. He has discovered that his own brain is both a broadcasting, and a receiving station for the vibration of thought, and he is beginning now to learn how to make practical use of this discovery. He has increased the speed of locomotion, until he may now travel at a speed of more than three hundred miles an hour. The time will soon come when a man may breakfast in New York, and lunch in San Francisco.

Man's only imagination, within reason, lies in his development and use of his imagination. He has not yet reached the apex of development in the use of his imaginative faculty. He has merely discovered that he has an imagination, and has commenced to use it in a very elementary way.

Two Forms of Imagination

The imaginative faculty functions in two forms. One is known as 'synthetic imagination,'' and the other as 'creative imagination.'

Synthetic Imagination: Through this faculty, one may arrange old concepts, ideas, or plans into new combinations. This faculty *creates* nothing. It merely works with the material of experience, education, and observation with which it is fed. It is the faculty used most by the inventor, with the exception of the 'genius' who draws upon the creative imagination, when he cannot solve his problem through synthetic imagination.

Creative Imagination: Through the faculty of creative imagination, the finite mind of man has direct communication with Infinite Intelligence. It is the faculty through which 'hunches' and 'inspirations' are received. It is by this faculty that all basic, or new ideas are handed over to man. It is through this faculty that thought vibrations from the minds of others are received. It is through this faculty that one individual may 'tune in,' or communicate with the subconscious minds of other men.

The creative imagination works automatically, in the manner described in subsequent pages. This faculty functions only when the conscious mind is vibrating at an exceedingly rapid rate, as for example, when the conscious mind is stimulated through the emotion of a *strong desire*.

The creative faculty becomes more alert, more receptive to vibrations from the sources mentioned, in proportion to its development through USE. This statement is significant! Ponder over it before passing on.

Keep in mind as you follow these principles, that the entire story of how one may convert desire into money cannot be told in one statement. The story will be complete, only when one has mastered, assimilated, and begun to make use of all the principles.

The great leaders of business, industry, finance, and the great artists, musicians, poets, and writers became great, because they developed the faculty of creative imagination.

Both the synthetic and creative faculties of imagination become more alert with use, just as any muscle or organ of the body develops through use.

Desire is only a thought, an impulse. It is nebulous and ephemeral. It is abstract, and of no value, until it has been transformed into its physical counterpart. While the synthetic imagination is the one which will be used most frequently, in the process of transforming the impulse of desire into money, you must keep in mind the fact, that you may face circumstances and situations which demand use of the creative imagination as well.

Your imaginative faculty may have become weak through inaction. It can be revived and made alert through use. This faculty does not die, though it may become quiescent through lack of use.

Centre your attention, for the time being, on the development of the synthetic imagination, because this is the faculty which you will use more often in the process of converting desire into money.

Transformation of the intangible impulse, of desire, into the tangible reality, of money, calls for the use of a plan, or plans. These plans must be formed with the aid of the imagination, and mainly, with the synthetic faculty.

Read the entire book through, then come back to this chapter, and begin at once to put your imagination to work on the building of a plan, or plans, for the transformation of your desire into money. Detailed instructions for the building of plans have been given in almost every chapter. Carry out the instructions best suited to your needs, reduce your plan to writing, if you have not already done so. The moment you complete this, you will have definitely given concrete form to the intangible desire. Read the preceding sentence once more. Read it aloud, very slowly, and as you do so, remember that the moment you reduce the statement of your desire, and a plan for its realisation, to writing, you have actually taken the first of a series of steps, which will enable you to convert the thought into its physical counterpart.

The earth on which you live, you, yourself, and every other material thing are the result of evolutionary change, through which microscopic bits of matter have been organised and arranged in an orderly fashion.

Moreover—and this statement is of stupendous importance—this earth, every one of the billions of individual cells of your body, and every atom of matter, *began as an intangible form of energy.*

Desire is thought impulse! Thought impulses are forms of energy. When you begin with the thought impulse, desire, to accumulate money, you are drafting into your service the same 'stuff' that Nature used in creating this earth, and every material form in the universe, including the body and brain in which the thought impulses function.

As far as science has been able to determine, the entire universe consists of but two elements—matter and energy.

Through the combination of energy and matter, has been created everything perceptible to man, from the largest star which floats in the heavens, down to, and including man, himself.

You are now engaged in the task of trying to profit by Nature's method. You are (sincerely and earnestly, we hope), trying to adapt yourself to Nature's laws, by endeavouring to convert desire into its physical or monetary equivalent. You can do it! It has been done before!

You can build a fortune through the aid of laws which are immutable. But, first, you must become familiar with these laws, and learn to use them. Through repetition, and by approaching the description of these principles from every conceivable angle, the author hopes to reveal to you the secret through which every great fortune has been accumulated.

Strange and paradoxical as it may seem, the 'secret' is not a secret. Nature, herself, advertises it in the earth on which we live, the stars, the planets suspended within our view, in the elements above and around us, in every blade of grass, and every form of life within our vision.

Nature advertises this 'secret' in the terms of biology, in the conversion of a tiny cell, so small that it may be lost on the point of a pin, into the human being now reading this line.

The conversion of desire into its physical equivalent is, certainly, no more miraculous!

Do not become discouraged if you do not fully comprehend all that has been stated. Unless you have long been a student of the mind, it is not to be expected that you will assimilate all that is in this chapter upon a first reading.

But you will, in time, make good progress.

The principles which follow will open the way for understanding of imagination. Assimilate that which you understand, as you read this philosophy for the first time, then, when you reread and study it, you will discover that something has happened to clarify it, and give you a broader understanding of the whole. Above all, do not stop, nor hesitate in your study of these principles until you have read the book at least three times, for then, you will not want to stop.

How to Make Practical use of Imagination?

Ideas are the beginning points of all fortunes. Ideas are products of the imagination. Let us examine a few well known ideas which have yielded huge fortunes, with the hope that these illustrations will convey definite information concerning the method by which imagination may be used in accumulating riches.

The Enchanted Kettle

Fifty years ago, an old country doctor drove to town, hitched his horse, quietly slipped into a drug store by the back door, and began 'dickering' with the young drug clerk.

His mission was destined to yield great wealth to many people. It was destined to bring to the South the most far-flung benefit since the Civil War.

For more than an hour, behind the prescription counter, the old doctor and the clerk talked in low tones. Then the doctor left. He went out to the buggy and brought back a large, old fashioned kettle, a big wooden paddle (used for stirring the contents of the kettle), and deposited them in the back of the store.

The clerk inspected the kettle, reached into his inside pocket, took out a roll of bills, and handed it over to the doctor. The roll contained exactly $500.00–the clerk's entire savings!

The doctor handed over a small slip of paper on which was written a secret formula. The words on that small slip of paper were worth a King's ransom! But not to the *doctor!* Those magic words were needed to start the kettle to boiling, but neither the doctor nor the young clerk knew what fabulous fortunes were destined to flow from that kettle.

The old doctor was glad to sell the outfit for five hundred dollars. The money would pay off his debts, and give him freedom of mind. The clerk was taking a big chance by staking his entire life's savings on a mere scrap of paper and an old kettle! He never dreamed his investment would start a kettle to overflowing with gold that would surpass the miraculous performance of Aladdin's lamp.

What the clerk *really purchased* was an idea!

The old kettle and the wooden paddle, and the secret message on a slip of paper were incidental. The strange performance of that kettle began to take place after the new owner mixed with the secret instructions an ingredient of which the doctor knew nothing.

READ THIS STORY carefully, give your imagination a test! See if you can discover what it was that the young man added to the secret message, which caused the kettle to overflow with gold. Remember, as you read, that this is not a story from Arabian Nights. Here you have a story of facts, stranger than fiction, facts which began in the form of an idea.

Let us take a look at the vast fortunes of gold this idea has produced. It has paid, and still pays huge fortunes to men and women all over the world, who distribute the contents of the kettle to millions of people.

The Old Kettle is now one of the world's largest consumers of sugar, thus providing jobs of a permanent nature to thousands of men and women engaged in growing sugar cane, and in refining and marketing sugar.

The Old Kettle consumes, annually, millions of glass bottles, providing jobs to huge numbers of glass workers.

The Old Kettle gives employment to an army of clerks, stenographers, copy writers, and advertising experts throughout the nation. It has brought fame and fortune to scores of artists who have created magnificent pictures describing the product.

The Old Kettle has converted a small Southern city into the business capital of the South, where it now benefits, directly, or indirectly, every business and practically every resident of the city.

The influence of this idea now benefits every civilised country in the world, pouring out a continuous stream of gold to all who touch it.

Gold from the kettle built and maintains one of the most prominent colleges of the South, where thousands of young people receive the training essential for success.

The Old Kettle has done other marvellous things.

All through the world depression, when factories, banks and business houses were folding up and quitting by the thousands, the owner of this Enchanted Kettle went marching on, *giving continuous employment* to an army of men and women all over the world, and paying out extra portions of gold to those who, long ago, *had faith in the idea.*

If the product of that old brass kettle could talk, it would tell thrilling tales of romance in every language. Romances of love, romances of business, romances of professional men and women who are daily being stimulated by it.

The author is sure of at least one such romance, for he was a part of it, and it all began not far from the very spot on which the drug clerk purchased the old kettle. It was here that the author met his wife, and it was she who first told him of the Enchanted Kettle. It was the product of that Kettle they were drinking when he asked her to accept him 'for better or worse.'

Now that you know the content of the Enchanted Kettle is a world famous drink, it is fitting that the author confess that the home city of the drink supplied him with a wife, also that the drink itself provides him with *stimulation of thought without intoxication*, and thereby it serves to give the refreshment of mind which an author must have to do his best work.

Whoever you are, wherever you may live, whatever occupation you may be engaged in, just remember in the future, every time you see the words 'Coca-Cola,' that its vast empire of wealth and influence grew out of a single idea, and that the mysterious ingredient the drug clerk—As a Candler—mixed with the secret formula was ...imagination!

Stop and think of that, for a moment.

Remember, also, that the thirteen steps to riches, described in this book, were the media through which the influence of Coca-Cola has been extended to every city, town, village, and cross-roads of the world, and that any idea you may create, as *sound and meritorious* as Coca-Cola, has the possibility of duplicating the stupendous record of this world-wide thirst-killer.

Truly, thoughts are things, and their scope of operation is the world, itself.

What I Would do if I had a Million Dollars

This story proves the truth of that old saying, 'where there's a will, there's a way.' It was told to me by that beloved educator and clergyman, the late Frank W. Gunsaulus, who began his preaching career in the stockyards region of South Chicago.

While Dr Gunsaulus was going through college, he observed many defects in our educational system, defects which he believed he could correct, if he were the head of a college. His *deepest desire* was to become the directing head of an educational institution in which young men and women would be taught to 'learn by doing.'

He made up his mind to organise a new college in which he could carry out his ideas, without being handicapped by orthodox methods of education.

He needed a million dollars to put the project across! Where was he to lay his hands on so large a sum of money?

The story of practically every great fortune starts with the day when a creator of ideas and a seller of ideas got together and worked in harmony. Carnegie surrounded himself with men who could do all that he could not do. Men who created ideas, and men who put ideas into operation, and made himself and the others fabulously rich.

Millions of people go through life hoping for favourable 'breaks.' Perhaps a favourable break can get one an opportunity, but the safest plan is not to depend upon luck. It was a favourable 'break' that gave me the biggest opportunity of my life--but--twenty-five years of *determined effort* had to be devoted to that opportunity before it became an asset.

The 'break' consisted of my good fortune in meeting and gaining the cooperation of Andrew Carnegie. On that occasion Carnegie planted in my mind the *idea* of organising the principles of achievement into a philosophy of success. Thousands of people have profited by the discoveries made in the twenty-five years of research, and several fortunes have been accumulated through the application of the philosophy. The beginning was simple. It was an IDEA which anyone might have developed.

The favourable break came through Carnegie, but what about the determination, definiteness of purpose, and the desire to attain the goal, and the persistent effort of twenty-five years? It was no ordinary desire that survived disappointment, discouragement, temporary defeat, criticism, and the constant reminding of 'waste of time.' It was a burning desire! An obsession!

When the idea was first planted in my mind by Mr Carnegie, it was coaxed, nursed, and enticed to *remain alive*. Gradually, the idea became a giant under its own power, and it coaxed, nursed, and drove me. Ideas are like that. First you give life and action and guidance to ideas, then they take on power of their own and sweep aside all opposition.

Ideas are intangible forces, but they have more power than the physical brains that give birth to them. They have the power to live on, after the brain that creates them has returned to dust. For example, take the power of Christianity. That began with a simple idea, born in the brain of Christ. Its chief tenet was, 'do unto others as you would have others do unto you.' Christ has gone back to the source from whence He came, but His idea goes marching on. Someday, it may grow up, and come into its own, then it will have fulfilled Christ's deepest desire. The idea has been developing only two thousand years. Give it time!

Organised Planning

The Crystallisation of Desire into Action

You have learned that everything man creates or acquires, begins in the form of desire, that desire is taken on the first lap of its journey, from the abstract to the concrete, into the workshop of the imagination, where plans for its transition are created and organised.

In Chapter two, you were instructed to take six definite, practical steps, as your first move in translating the desire for money into its monetary equivalent. One of these steps is the formation of a definite, practical plan, or plans, through which this transformation may be made.

You will now be instructed how to build plans which will be practical, viz:

(a) Ally yourself with a group of as many people as you may need for the creation, and carrying out of your plan, or plans for the accumulation of money--making use of the 'Master Mind' principle described in a later chapter. (Compliance with this instruction is absolutely essential. Do not neglect it.)

(b) Before forming your 'Master Mind' alliance, decide what advantages, and benefits, you may offer the individual members of your group, in return for their cooperation. No one will work indefinitely without some form of compensation. No intelligent person will either request or expect another to work without adequate compensation, although this may not always be in the form of money.

(c) Arrange to meet with the members of your 'Master Mind' group at least twice a week, and more often if possible, until you have jointly perfected the necessary plan, or plans for the accumulation of money.

(d) Maintain perfect harmony between yourself and every member of your 'Master Mind' group. If you fail to carry out this instruction to the letter, you may expect to meet with failure. The 'Master Mind' principle *cannot* obtain where perfect harmony does not prevail.

Facts to keep in mind

First. You are engaged in an undertaking of major importance to you. To be sure of success, you must have plans which are faultless.

Second. You must have the advantage of the experience, education, native ability and imagination of other minds. This is in harmony with the methods followed by every person who has accumulated a great fortune.

No individual has sufficient experience, education, native ability, and knowledge to insure the accumulation of a great fortune, without the cooperation of other people. Every plan you adopt, in your endeavour to accumulate wealth, should be the joint creation of yourself and every other member of your 'Master Mind' group. You may originate your own plans, either in whole or in part, but see that those plans are checked, and approved by the members of your 'master mind' alliance.

If the first plan which you adopt does not work successfully, replace it with a new plan, if this new plan fails to work, replace it, in turn with still another, and so on, until you find a plan which does work. Right here is the point at which the majority of men meet with failure, because of their lack of persistence in creating new plans to take the place of those which fail.

The most intelligent man living cannot succeed in accumulating money—nor in any other undertaking—without plans which are practical and workable. Just keep this fact in mind, and remember when your plans fail, that temporary defeat is not permanent failure. It may only mean that your plans have not been sound. Build other plans. Start all over again.

Thomas A Edison 'failed' ten thousand times before he perfected the incandescent electric light bulb. That is—he met with *temporary defeat* ten thousand times, before his efforts were crowned with success.

Temporary defeat should mean only one thing, the certain knowledge that there is something wrong with your plan. Millions of men go through life in misery and poverty, because they lack a sound plan through which to accumulate a fortune.

Henry Ford accumulated a fortune, not because of his superior mind, but because he adopted and followed a plan which proved to be sound. A thousand men could be pointed out, each with a better education than Ford's, yet each of whom lives in poverty, because he does not possess the right plan for the accumulation of money.

Your achievement can be no greater than your plans are sound. That may seem to be an axiomatic statement, but it is true. Samuel Insull lost his fortune of over one hundred million dollars. The Insull fortune was built on plans which were sound. The business depression forced Mr Insull to change his plans; and the change brought 'temporary defeat,' because his new plans were not sound. Mr Insull is now an old man, he may, consequently, accept 'failure' instead of 'temporary defeat,' but if his experience turns out to be failure, it will be for the reason that he lacks the fire of persistence to rebuild his plans.

No man is ever whipped, until he quits—*in his own mind.*

This fact will be repeated many times, because it is so easy to 'take the count' at the first sign of defeat.

James J Hill met with temporary defeat when he first endeavoured to raise the necessary capital to build a railroad from the East to the West, but he, too turned defeat into victory *through new plans.*

Henry Ford met with temporary defeat, not only at the beginning of his automobile career, but after he had gone far toward the top. He created new plans, and went marching on to financial victory.

We see men who have accumulated great fortunes, but we often recognise only their triumph, overlooking the temporary defeats which they had to surmount before 'arriving.'

No follower of this philosophy can reasonably expect to accumulate a fortune without experiencing temporary defeat.

When defeat comes, accept it as a signal that your plans are not sound, rebuild those plans, and set sail once more toward your coveted goal. If you give up before your goal has been reached, you are a 'quitter.' A quitter never wins-and-a winner never quits. Lift this sentence out, write it on a piece of paper in letters an inch high, and place it where you will see it every night before you go to sleep, and every morning before you go to work.

When you begin to select members for your 'Mastermind' group, strive to select those who do not take defeat seriously.

Some people foolishly believe that only money can make money. This is not true! Desire, transmuted into its monetary equivalent, through the principles laid down here, is the agency through which money is 'made.' Money, of itself, is nothing but inert matter. It cannot move, think, or talk, but it can 'hear' when a man who desires it, calls it to come!

Planning the Sale of Services

The remainder of this chapter has been given over to a description of ways and means of marketing personal services. The information here conveyed will be of practical help to any person having any form of personal services to market, but it will be of priceless benefit to those who aspire to leadership in their chosen occupations.

Intelligent planning is essential for success in any undertaking designed to accumulate riches. Here will be found detailed instructions to those who must begin the accumulation of riches by selling personal services.

It should be encouraging to know that practically all the great fortunes began in the form of compensation for personal services, or from the sale of ideas. What else, except ideas and personal services, would one not possessed of property have to give in return for riches?

Broadly speaking, there are two types of people in the world. One type is known as leaders, and the other as followers. Decide at the outset whether you intend to become a leader in your chosen calling, or remain a follower. The difference in compensation is vast. The follower cannot reasonably expect the compensation to which a leader is entitled, although many followers make the mistake of expecting such pay.

It is no disgrace to be a follower. On the other hand, it is no credit to remain a follower. Most great leaders began in the capacity of followers. They became great leaders because they were intelligent followers. With few exceptions, the man who cannot follow a leader intelligently, cannot become an efficient leader. The man who can follow a leader most efficiently, is usually the man who develops into leadership most rapidly. An intelligent follower has many advantages, among them the opportunity to acquire knowledge from his leader.

The Major Attributes of Leadership

Unwavering Courage: Based upon knowledge of self, and of one's occupation. No follower wishes to be dominated by a leader who lacks self-confidence and courage. No intelligent follower will be dominated by such a leader very long.

Self-control: The man who cannot control himself, can never control others. Self-control sets a mighty example for one's followers, which the more intelligent will emulate.

A keen sense of justice: Without a sense of fairness and justice, no leader can command and retain the respect of his followers.

Definiteness of decision: The man who wavers in his decisions, shows that he is not sure of himself. He cannot lead others successfully.

Definiteness of plans: The successful leader must plan his work, and *work his plan*. A leader who moves by guesswork, without practical, definite plans, is comparable to a ship without a rudder. Sooner or later he will land on the rocks.

The habit of doing more than paid for: One of the penalties of leadership is the necessity of willingness, upon the part of the leader, to do more than he requires of his followers.

A pleasing personality: No slovenly, careless person can become a successful leader. Leadership calls for respect. Followers will not respect a leader who does not grade high on all of the factors of a Pleasing Personality.

Sympathy and understanding: The successful leader must be in sympathy with his followers. Moreover, he must understand them and their problems.

Mastery of detail: Successful leadership calls for mastery of details of the leader's position.

Willingness to take full responsibility: The successful leader must be willing to assume responsibility for the mistakes and the shortcomings of his followers. If he tries to shift this responsibility, he will not remain the leader. If one of his followers makes a mistake, and shows himself incompetent, the leader must consider that it is *he* who failed.

Cooperation: The successful leader must understand, and *apply* the principle of cooperative effort and be able to induce his followers to do the same. Leadership calls for power, and power calls for cooperation.

There are two forms of leadership. The first, and by far the most effective, is Leadership of Consent, and with the sympathy of the followers. The second is Leadership of Force, without the consent and sympathy of the followers.

History is filled with evidences that Leadership by Force cannot endure. The downfall and disappearance of 'Dictators' and kings is significant. It means that people will not follow forced leadership indefinitely.

The world has just entered a new era of relationship between leaders and followers, which very clearly calls for new leaders, and a new brand of leadership in business and industry. Those who belong to the old school of leadership by force, must acquire an understanding of the new brand of leadership (cooperation) or be relegated to the rank and file of the followers. There is no other way out for them.

The relationship of employer and employee, or of leader and follower, in the future, will be one of mutual cooperation, based upon an equitable division of the profits of business. In the future, the relationship of employer and employee will be more like a partnership than it has been in the past.

Napoleon, Kaiser Wilhelm of Germany, the Czar of Russia, and the King of Spain were examples of leadership by force. Their leadership passed. Without much difficulty, one might point to the prototypes of these ex-leaders, among the business, financial, and labour leaders of America who have been dethroned or slated to go. *Leadership-by-consent* of the followers is the only brand which can endure!

Men may follow the forced leadership temporarily, but they will not do so willingly.

The new brand of leadership will embrace the eleven factors of leadership, described in this chapter, as well as some other factors. The man who makes these the basis of his leadership, will find abundant opportunity to lead in any walk of life. The depression was prolonged, largely, because the world lacked leadership of the new brand. At the end of the depression, the demand for leaders who are competent to apply the new methods of leadership has greatly exceeded the supply. Some of the old type of leaders will reform and adapt themselves to the new brand of leadership, but generally speaking, the world will have to look for new timber for its leadership.

This necessity may be your opportunity!

⌂ ⌂ ⌂

Persistence

The Sustained Effort to Induce Faith

Persistence is an essential factor in the procedure of transmuting desire into its monetary equivalent. The basis of persistence is the power of will.

Will-power and desire, when properly combined, make an irresistible pair. Men who accumulate great fortunes are generally known as cold-blooded, and sometimes ruthless. Often they are misunderstood. What they have is will-power, which they mix with persistence, and place back of their desires to insure the attainment of their objectives.

Henry Ford has been generally misunderstood to be ruthless and cold-blooded. This misconception grew out of Ford's habit of following through in all of his plans with persistence

The majority of people are ready to throw their aims and purposes overboard, and give up at the first sign of opposition or misfortune. A few carry on despite all opposition, until they attain their goal. These few are the Fords, Carnegies, Rockefellers, and Edisons.

There may be no heroic connotation to the word 'persistence,' but the quality is to the character of man what carbon is to steel.

The building of a fortune, generally, involves the application of the entire thirteen factors of this philosophy. These principles must be understood; they must be applied with persistence by all who accumulate money.

If you are following this book with the intention of applying the knowledge it conveys, your first test as to your persistence will come when you begin to follow the six steps described in the second chapter. Unless you are one of the two out of every hundred who already have a definite goal at which you are aiming, and a definite plan for its attainment, you may read the instructions, and then pass on with your daily routine, and never comply with those instructions.

The author is checking you up at this point, because lack of persistence is one of the major causes of failure. Moreover, experience with thousands of people has proved that lack of persistence is a weakness common to the majority of men. It is a weakness which may be overcome by effort. The ease with which lack of persistence may be conquered will depend *entirely* upon the intensity of one's desire.

The starting point of all achievement is desire. Keep this constantly in mind. Weak desires bring weak results, just as a small amount of fire makes a small amount of heat. If you find yourself lacking in persistence, this weakness may be remedied by building a stronger fire under your desires.

Continue to read through to the end, then go back to previous section, and start *immediately* to carry out the instructions given in connection with the six steps. The eagerness with which you follow these instructions will indicate clearly, how much, or how little you really desire to accumulate money. If you find that you are indifferent, you may be sure that you have not yet acquired the 'money consciousness' which you must possess, before you can be sure of accumulating a fortune.

Fortunes gravitate to men whose minds have been prepared to 'attract' them, just as surely as water gravitates to the ocean. In this book may be found all the stimuli necessary to 'attune' any normal mind to the vibrations which will attract the object of one's desires.

If you find you are weak in persistence, centre your attention upon the instructions contained in the chapter on 'Power'; surround yourself with 'Masterminds' group, and through the cooperative efforts of the members of this group, you can develop persistence. You will find additional instructions for the development of persistence in the chapters on auto-suggestion, and the subconscious mind. Follow the instructions outlined in these chapters until your habit nature hands over to your subconscious mind, a clear picture of the object of your desire. From that point on, you will not be handicapped by lack of persistence.

Your subconscious mind works continuously, while you are awake, and while you are asleep.

Spasmodic, or occasional effort to apply the rules will be of no value to you. To get results, you must apply all of the rules until their application becomes a fixed habit with you. In no other way can you develop the necessary 'money consciousness.'

Poverty is attracted to the one whose mind is favourable

to it, as money is attracted to him whose mind has been deliberately prepared to attract it, and through the same laws. Poverty consciousness will voluntarily seize the mind which is not occupied with the money consciousness. A poverty consciousness develops without *conscious* application of habits favourable to it. The money consciousness must be created to order, unless one is born with such a consciousness.

Catch the full significance of the statements in the preceding paragraph, and you will understand the importance of persistence in the accumulation of a fortune. Without persistence, you will be defeated, even before you start. With persistence you will win.

If you have ever experienced a nightmare, you will realize the value of persistence. You are lying in bed, half awake, with a feeling that you are about to smother. You are unable to turn over, or to move a muscle. You realise that you must begin to regain control over your muscles. Through persistent effort of will-power, you finally manage to move the fingers of one hand. By continuing to move your fingers, you extend your control to the muscles of one arm, until you can lift it. Then you gain control of the other arm in the same manner. You finally gain control over the muscles of one leg, and then extend it to the other leg. Then--with one supreme effort of will--you regain complete control over your muscular system, and "snap 'out of your nightmare. The trick has been turned step by step.

You may find it necessary to 'snap' out of your mental inertia, through a similar procedure, moving slowly at first, then increasing your speed, until you gain complete control over your will. Be persistent no matter how slowly you may, at first, have to move. With persistence will come success.

If you select your 'Master Mind' group with care, you will have at least one person who will aid you in the development of persistence. Some men who have accumulated great fortunes, did so because of necessity. They developed the habit of persistence, because they were so closely driven by circumstances, that they *had to become persistent.*

There is no substitute for Persistence! It cannot be supplanted by any other quality! Remember this, and it will hearten you, in the beginning, when the going may seem difficult and slow.

Those who have cultivated the habit of persistence seem to enjoy insurance against failure. No matter how many times they are defeated, they finally arrive up toward the top of the ladder. Sometimes it appears that there is a hidden Guide whose duty is to test men through all sorts of discouraging experiences. Those who pick themselves up after defeat and keep on trying, arrive; and the world cries, 'Bravo! I knew you could do it!' The hidden guide lets no one enjoy great achievement without passing the persistence test. Those who can't take it, simply do not make the grade.

Those who can 'take it' are bountifully rewarded for their persistence. They receive, as their compensation, whatever goal they are pursuing. That is not all! They receive something infinitely more important than material compensation—the knowledge that 'Every failure brings with it the seed of an equivalent advantage.'

There are exceptions to this rule; a few people know from experience the soundness of persistence. They are the ones who have not accepted defeat as being anything more than temporary. They are the ones whose desires are so persistently applied that defeat is finally changed into victory. We who stand on the side-lines of life see the overwhelmingly large number who go down in defeat, never to rise again. We see the few who take the punishment of defeat as an urge to greater effort. These, fortunately, never learn to accept life's reverse gear. But what we do not see, what most of us never suspect of existing, is the silent but irresistible power which comes to the rescue of those who fight on in the face of discouragement. If we speak of this power at all we call it persistence, and let it go at that. One thing we all know, if one does not possess persistence, one does not achieve noteworthy success in any calling.

As these lines are being written, I look up from my work, and see before me, less than a block away, the great mysterious 'Broadway,' the 'Graveyard of Dead Hopes,' and the 'Front Porch of Opportunity.' From all over the world people have come to Broadway, seeking fame, fortune, power, love, or whatever it is that human beings call success. Once in a great while someone steps out from the long procession of seekers, and the world hears that another person has mastered Broadway. But Broadway is not easily nor quickly conquered. She acknowledges talent, recognizes genius, pays off in money, only after one has refused to quit.

Then we know he has discovered the secret of how to conquer Broadway. The secret is always inseparably attached to one word, persistence!

SECTION TWO

THE SCIENCE OF GETTING RICH
by Wallace D Wattles

'If you want to help the poor, demonstrate to
them that they can become rich; prove it by
getting rich yourself.'

The Right to be Rich

Whatever may be said in praise of poverty, the fact remains that it is not possible to live a really complete or successful life unless one is rich. No man can rise to his greatest possible height in talent or soul development unless he has plenty of money; for to unfold the soul and to develop talent he must have many things to use, and he cannot have these things unless he has money to buy them with.

Man develops in mind, soul, and body by making use of things, and society is so organised that man must have money in order to become the possessor of things; therefore, the basis of all advancement for man must be the science of getting rich.

The object of all life is development; and everything that lives has an inalienable right to all the development it is capable of attaining.

Man's right to life means his right to have the free and unrestricted use of all the things which may be necessary to his fullest mental, spiritual, and physical unfoldment; or, in other words, his right to be rich.

In this book, I shall not speak of riches in a figurative way; to be really rich does not mean to be satisfied or contented with a little. No man ought to be satisfied with a little if he is capable of using and enjoying more. The purpose of Nature is the advancement and unfoldment of life; and every man should have all that can contribute to the power, elegance, beauty, and richness of life; to be content with less is sinful.

The man who owns all he wants for the living of all the life he is capable of living is rich; and no man who has not plenty of money can have all he wants. Life has advanced so far, and become so complex, that even the most ordinary man or woman requires a great amount of wealth in order to live in a manner that even approaches completeness. Every person naturally wants to become all that he is capable of becoming; this desire to realise innate possibilities is inherent in human nature; we cannot help wanting to be all that we can be. Success in life is becoming what you want to be; you can become what you want to be only by making use of things, and you can have the free use of things only as you become rich enough to buy them. To understand the science of getting rich is therefore the most essential of all knowledge.

There is nothing wrong in wanting to get rich. The desire for riches is really the desire for a richer, fuller, and more abundant life; and that desire is praiseworthy. The man who does not desire to live more abundantly is abnormal, and so the man who does not desire to have money enough to buy all he wants is abnormal.

There are three motives for which we live; we live for the body, we live for the mind, and we live for the soul. No one of these is better or holier than the other; all are alike desirable, and no one of the three—body, mind, or soul—can live fully if either of the others is cut short of full life and expression. It is not right or noble to live only for the soul and deny mind or body; and it is wrong to live for the intellect and deny body and soul.

We are all acquainted with the loathsome consequences of living for the body and denying both mind and soul; and we see that real life means the complete expression of all that man can give forth through body, mind, and soul. Whatever he may say, no man can be really happy or satisfied unless his body is living fully in every function, and unless the same is true of his mind and his soul. Wherever there is unexpressed possibility, or function not performed, there is unsatisfied desire. Desire is possibility seeking expression, or function seeking performance.

Man cannot live fully in body without good food, comfortable clothing, and warm shelter; and without freedom from excessive toil. Rest and recreation are also necessary to his physical life.

He cannot live fully in mind without books and time to study without opportunity for travel and observation, or without intellectual companionship.

To live fully in mind, he must have intellectual recreations, and must surround himself with all the objects of art and beauty he is capable of using and appreciating.

To live fully in soul, man must have love; and love is denied expression by poverty.

Man's highest happiness is found in the bestowal of benefits on those he loves; love finds its most natural and spontaneous expression in giving. The man who has nothing to give cannot fill his place as a husband or father, as a citizen, or as a man. It is in the use of material things that man finds full life for his body, develops his mind, and unfolds his soul. It is therefore of supreme importance to him that he should be rich.

It is perfectly right that you should desire to be rich; if you are a normal man or woman you cannot help doing so. It is perfectly right that you should give your best attention to the Science of Getting Rich, for it is the noblest and most necessary of all studies. If you neglect this study, you are derelict in your duty to yourself, to God, and to humanity; for you can render God and humanity no greater service than to make the most of yourself.

There is a Science to Getting Rich

There is a science of getting rich, and it is an exact science, like algebra or arithmetic. There are certain laws which govern the process of acquiring riches; once these laws are learned and obeyed by any man, he will get rich with mathematical certainty. There is a science to getting rich.

The ownership of money and property comes as a result of doing things in a certain way; those who do things in this Certain Way, whether on purpose or accidentally, get rich; while those who do not do things in this Certain Way, no matter how hard they work or how able they are, remain poor.

It is a natural law that like causes always produce like effects; and, therefore, any man or woman who learns to do things in this Certain Way will infallibly get rich.

That the above statement is true is shown by the following facts:

Getting rich is not a matter of environment, for, if it

were, all the people in certain neighbourhoods would become wealthy; the people of one city would all be rich, while those of other towns would all be poor; or the inhabitants of one state would roll in wealth, while those of an adjoining state would be in poverty.

But everywhere we see rich and poor living side by side, in the same environment, and often engaged in the same vocations. When two men are in the same locality, and in the same business, and one gets rich while the other remains poor, it shows that getting rich is not, primarily, a matter of environment. Some environments may be more favourable than others, but when two men in the same business are in the same neighbourhood, and one gets rich while the other fails, it indicates that getting rich is the result of doing things in a Certain Way.

And further, the ability to do things in this Certain Way is not due solely to the possession of talent, for many people who have great talent remain poor, while others who have very little talent get rich.

Studying the people who have got rich, we find that they are an average lot in all respects, having no greater talents and abilities than other men. It is evident that they do not get rich because they possess talents and abilities that other men have not, but because they happen to do things in a Certain Way.

Getting rich is not the result of saving, or 'thrift'; many very penurious people are poor, while free spenders often get rich. Nor is getting rich due to doing things which others fail to do; for two men in the same business often do almost exactly the same things, and one gets rich while the other remains poor or becomes a bankrupt.

From all these things, we must come to the conclusion that getting rich is the result of doing things in a Certain Way.

If getting rich is the result of doing things in a Certain Way, and if like causes always produce like effects, then any man or woman who can do things in that way can become rich, and the whole matter is brought within the domain of exact science.

The question arises here, whether this Certain Way may not be so difficult that only a few may follow it. This cannot be true, as we have seen, so far as natural ability is concerned. Talented people get rich, and blockheads get rich; intellectually brilliant people get rich, and very stupid people get rich; physically strong people get rich, and weak and sickly people get rich.

Some degree of ability to think and understand is, of course, essential; but in so far as natural ability is concerned, any man or woman who has sense enough to read and understand these words can certainly get rich.

Also, we have seen that it is not a matter of environment. Location counts for something; one would not go to the heart of the Sahara and expect to do successful business.

Getting rich involves the necessity of dealing with men, and of being where there are people to deal with; and if these people are inclined to deal in the way you want to deal, so much the better. But that is about as far as environment goes.

If anybody else in your town can get rich, so can you; and if anybody else in your state can get rich, so can you.

Again, it is not a matter of choosing some particular business or profession. People get rich in every business, and in every profession; while their next door neighbours in the same vocation remain in poverty.

It is true that you will do best in a business which you like, and which is congenial to you; and if you have certain talents which are well developed, you will do best in a business which calls for the exercise of those talents.

Also, you will do best in a business which is suited to your locality; an ice-cream parlour would do better in a warm climate than in Greenland, and a salmon fishery will succeed better in the Northwest than in Florida, where there are no salmon.

But, aside from these general limitations, getting rich is not dependent upon your engaging in some particular business, but upon your learning to do things in a Certain Way. If you are now in business, and anybody else in your locality is getting rich in the same business, while you are *not* getting rich, it is because you are not doing things in the same way that the other person is doing them.

No one is prevented from getting rich by lack of capital. True, as you get capital the increase becomes more easy and rapid; but one who has capital is already rich, and does not need to consider how to become so. No matter how poor you may be, if you begin to do things in the Certain Way you will begin to get rich; and you will begin to have capital. The getting of capital is a part of the process of getting rich; and it is a part of the result which invariably follows the doing of things in the Certain Way.

You may be the poorest man on the continent, and be deeply in debt; you may have neither friends, influence, nor resources; but if you begin to do things in this Way, you must infallibly begin to get rich, for like causes must produce like effects. If you have no capital, you can get capital; if you are in the wrong business, you can get into the right business; if you are in the wrong location, you can go to the right location; and you can do so *by beginning in your present business and in your present location* to do things in the Certain Way which causes success.

The Principle in the Science of Getting Rich

Thought is the only power which can produce tangible riches from the Formless Substance. The stuff from which all things are made is a substance which thinks, and a thought of form in this substance produces the form.

Original Substance moves according to its thoughts; every form and process you see in nature is the visible expression of a thought in Original Substance. As the Formless Stuff thinks of a form, it takes that form; as it thinks of a motion, it makes that motion. That is the way all things were created. We live in a thought world, which is part of a thought universe. The first principle in the science of getting rich

The thought of a moving universe extended throughout Formless Substance, and the Thinking Stuff moving according to that thought, took the form of systems of planets, and maintains that form. Thinking Substance takes the form of its thought, and moves according to the thought. Holding the idea of a circling system of suns and worlds, it takes the form of these bodies, and moves them as it thinks. Thinking the form of a slow-growing oak tree, it moves accordingly, and produces the tree, though centuries may be required to do the work. In creating, the Formless seems to move according to the lines of motion it has established; the thought of an oak tree does not cause the instant formation of a full-grown tree, but it does start in motion the forces which will produce the tree, along established lines of growth.

Every thought of form, held in thinking Substance, causes the creation of the form, but always, or at least generally, along lines of growth and action already established.

The thought of a house of a certain construction, if it were impressed upon Formless Substance, might not cause the instant formation of the house; but it would cause the turning of creative energies already working in trade and commerce into such channels as to result in the speedy building of the house. And if there were no existing channels through which the creative energy could work, then the house would be formed directly from primal substance, without waiting for the slow processes of the organic and inorganic world.

No thought of form can be impressed upon Original Substance without causing the creation of the form.

Man is a thinking centre, and can originate thought. All the forms that man fashions with his hands must first exist in his thought; he cannot shape a thing until he has thought that thing.

And so far man has confined his efforts wholly to the work of his hands; he has applied manual labour to the world of forms, seeking to change or modify those already existing. He has never thought of trying to cause the creation of new forms by impressing his thoughts upon Formless Substance.

When man has a thought-form, he takes material from the forms of nature, and makes an image of the form which is in his mind. He has, so far, made little or no effort to co-operate with Formless Intelligence; to work 'with the Father.'

He has not dreamed that he can 'do what he seeth the Father doing.' Man re-shapes and modifies existing forms by manual labour; he has given no attention to the question whether he may not produce things from Formless Substance by communicating his thoughts to it. We propose to prove that he may do so; to prove that any man or woman may do so, and to show how. As our first step, we must lay down three fundamental propositions.

First, we assert that there is one original formless stuff, or substance, from which all things are made. All the seemingly many elements are but different presentations of one element; all the many forms found in organic and inorganic nature are but different shapes, made from the same stuff. And this stuff is thinking stuff; a thought held in it produces the form of the thought. Thought, in thinking substance, produces shapes. Man is a thinking centre, capable of original thought; if man can communicate his thought to original thinking substance, he can cause the creation, or formation, of the thing he thinks about. To summarise this:

There is a thinking stuff from which all things are made, and which, in its original state, permeates, penetrates, and fills the interspaces of the universe.

A thought, in this substance, produces the thing that is imaged by the thought.

Man can form things in his thought, and, by impressing his thought upon formless substance, can cause the thing he thinks about to be created.

It may be asked if I can prove these statements; and without going into details, I answer that I can do so, both by logic and experience.

Reasoning back from the phenomena of form and thought, I come to one original thinking substance; and reasoning forward from this thinking substance, I come to man's power to cause the formation of the thing he thinks about.

And by experiment, I find the reasoning true; and this is my strongest proof.

If one man who reads this book gets rich by doing what it tells him to do, that is evidence in support of my claim; but if every man who does what it tells him to do gets rich, that is positive proof until someone goes through the process and fails. The theory is true until the process fails; and this process will not fail, for every man who does exactly what this book tells him to do will get rich.

I have said that men get rich by doing things in a Certain Way; and in order to do so, men must become able to think in a certain way.

A man's way of doing things is the direct result of the way he thinks about things.

To do things in the way you want to do them, you will have to acquire the ability to think the way you want to think; this is the first step toward getting rich.

To think what you want to think is to think Truth, regardless of appearances.

Every man has the natural and inherent power to think what he wants to think, but it requires far more effort to do so than it does to think the thoughts which are suggested by appearances. To think according to appearances is easy; to think truth regardless of appearances is laborious, and requires the expenditure of more power than any other work man is called upon to perform.

There is no labour from which most people shrink as they do from that of sustained and consecutive thought; it is the hardest work in the world. This is especially true when truth is contrary to appearances. Every appearance in the visible world tends to produce a corresponding form in the mind which observes it; and this can only be prevented by holding the thought of the Truth.

To look upon the appearance of disease will produce the form of disease in your own mind, and ultimately in your body, unless you hold the thought of the truth, which is that there is no disease; it is only an appearance, and the reality is health.

To look upon the appearances of poverty will produce corresponding forms in your own mind, unless you hold to the truth that there is no poverty; there is only abundance.

To think health when surrounded by the appearances of disease, or to think riches when in the midst of appearances of poverty, requires power; but he who acquires this power becomes a mastermind. He can conquer fate; he can have what he wants.

This power can only be acquired by getting hold of the basic fact which is behind all appearances; and that fact is that there is one Thinking Substance, from which and by which all things are made.

Then we must grasp the truth that every thought held in this substance becomes a form, and that man can so impress his thoughts upon It as to cause them to take form and become visible things.

When we realise this, we lose all doubt and fear, for we know that we can create what we want to create; we can get what we want to have, and can become what we want to be. As a first step toward getting rich, you must believe the three fundamental statements given previously in this chapter; and in order to emphasise them, I repeat them here:

There is a thinking stuff from which all things are made, and which, in its original state, permeates, penetrates, and fills the interspaces of the universe.

A thought, in this substance, produces the thing that is imaged by the thought.

Man can form things in his thought, and, by impressing his thought upon formless substance, can cause the thing he thinks about to be created.

You must lay aside all other concepts of the universe than this monistic one; and you must dwell upon this until it is fixed in your mind, and has become your habitual thought. Read these creed statements over and over again; fix every word upon your memory, and meditate upon them until you firmly believe what they say. If a doubt comes to you, cast it aside as a sin. Do not listen to arguments against this idea; do not go to churches or lectures where a contrary concept of things is taught or preached. Do not read magazines or books which teach a different idea; if you get mixed up in your faith, all your efforts will be in vain.

Do not ask why these things are true, nor speculate as to how they can be true; simply take them on trust.

The science of getting rich begins with the absolute acceptance of this faith.

How Riches Come Home to You

When I say that you do not have to drive sharp bargains, I do not mean that you do not have to drive any bargains at all, or that you are above the necessity for having any dealings with your fellow men. I mean that you will not need to deal with them unfairly; you do not have to get something for nothing, *but can give to every man more than you take from him.*

You cannot give every man more in cash market value than you take from him, but you can give him more in use value than the cash value of the thing you take from him.

The paper, ink, and other material in this book may not be worth the money you paid for it; but if the ideas suggested by it bring you thousands of dollars, you have not been wronged by those who sold it to you; they have given you a great use value for a small cash value.

Let us suppose that I own a picture by one of the great artists, which, in any civilized community, is worth thousands of dollars. I take it to Baffin Bay, and by 'salesmanship' induce an Eskimo to give a bundle of furs worth $500 for it. I have really wronged him, for he has no use for the picture; it has no use value to him; it will not add to his life.

But suppose I give him a gun worth $50 for his furs; then he has made a good bargain. He has use for the gun; it will get him many more furs and much food; it will add to his life in every way; it will make him rich.

When you rise from the competitive to the creative plane, you can scan your business transactions very strictly, and if you are selling any man anything which does not add more to his life than the thing he gives you in exchange, you can afford to stop it. You do not have to beat anybody in business.

And if you are in a business which does beat people, get out of it at once.

Give every man more in use value than you take from him in cash value; then you are adding to the life of the world by every business transaction.

If you have people working for you, you must take from them more in cash value than you pay them in wages; but you can so organise your business that it will be filled with the principle of advancement, and so that each employee who wishes to do so may advance a little every day.

You can make your business do for your employees what this book is doing for you. You can so conduct your business that it will be a sort of ladder, by which every employee who will take the trouble may climb to riches himself; and given the opportunity, if he will not do so it is not your fault.

And finally, because you are to cause the creation of your riches from Formless Substance which permeates all your environment, it does not follow that they are to take shape from the atmosphere and come into being before your eyes.

If you want a sewing machine, for instance, I do not mean to tell you that you are to impress the thought of a sewing machine on Thinking Substance until the machine is formed without hands, in the room where you sit, or elsewhere. But if you want a sewing machine, hold the mental image of it with the most positive certainty that it is being made, or is on its way to you. After once forming the thought, have the most absolute and unquestioning faith that the sewing machine is coming; never think of it, or speak of it, in any other way than as being sure to arrive. Claim it as already yours.

It will be brought to you by the power of the Supreme

Intelligence, acting upon the minds of men. If you live in Maine, it may be that a man will be brought from Texas or Japan to engage in some transaction which will result in your getting what you want.

If so, the whole matter will be as much to that man's advantage as it is to yours.

Do not forget for a moment that the Thinking Substance is through all, in all, communicating with all, and can influence all. The desire of Thinking Substance for fuller life and better living has caused the creation of all the sewing machines already made; and it can cause the creation of millions more, and will, whenever men set it in motion by desire and faith, and by acting in a Certain Way.

You can certainly have a sewing machine in your house; and it is just as certain that you can have any other thing or things which you want, and which you will use for the advancement of your own life and the lives of others.

You need not hesitate about asking largely; 'it is your Father's pleasure to give you the kingdom,' said Jesus.

Original Substance wants to live all that is possible in you, and wants you to have all that you can or will use for the living of the most abundant life.

If you fix upon your consciousness the fact that the desire you feel for the possession of riches is one with the desire of Omnipotence for more complete expression, your faith becomes invincible.

Once I saw a little boy sitting at a piano, and vainly trying to bring harmony out of the keys; and I saw that he was grieved and provoked by his inability to play real music. I asked him the cause of his vexation, and he answered, 'I can feel the music in me, but I can't make my hands go right.' The music in him was the URGE of Original Substance, containing all the possibilities of all life; all that there is of music was seeking expression through the child.

God, the One Substance, is trying to live and do and enjoy things through humanity. He is saying, 'I want hands to build wonderful structures, to play divine harmonies, to paint glorious pictures; I want feet to run my errands, eyes to see my beauties, tongues to tell mighty truths and to sing marvellous songs,' and so on.

All that there is of possibility is seeking expression through men. God wants those who can play music to have pianos and every other instrument, and to have the means to cultivate their talents to the fullest extent; He wants those who can appreciate beauty to be able to surround themselves with beautiful things; He wants those who can discern truth to have every opportunity to travel and observe; He wants those who can appreciate dress to be beautifully clothed, and those who can appreciate good food to be luxuriously fed.

He wants all these things because it is Himself that enjoys and appreciates them; it is God who wants to play, and sing, and enjoy beauty, and proclaim truth, and wear fine clothes, and eat good foods.

'It is God that worketh in you to will and to do,' said Paul.

The desire you feel for riches is the Infinite, seeking to express Himself in you as He sought to find expression in the little boy at the piano.

So you need not hesitate to ask largely.

Your part is to focalise and express the desires of God.

This is a difficult point with most people; they retain

something of the old idea that poverty and self-sacrifice are pleasing to God. They look upon poverty as a part of the plan, a necessity of nature. They have the idea that God has finished His work, and made all that He can make, and that the majority of men must stay poor because there is not enough to go around. They hold to so much of this erroneous thought that they feel ashamed to ask for wealth; they try not to want more than a very modest competence, just enough to make them fairly comfortable.

I recall now the case of one student who was told that he must get in mind a clear picture of the things he desired, so that the creative thought of them might be impressed on Formless Substance. He was a very poor man, living in a rented house, and having only what he earned from day to day; and he could not grasp the fact that all wealth was his. So, after thinking the matter over, he decided that he might reasonably ask for a new rug for the floor of his best room, and an anthracite coal stove to heat the house during the cold weather. Following the instructions given in this book, he obtained these things in a few months; and then it dawned upon him that he had not asked enough. He went through the house in which he lived, and planned all the improvements he would like to make in it; he mentally added a bay window here and a room there, until it was complete in his mind as his ideal home; and then he planned its furnishings.

Holding the whole picture in his mind, he began living in the Certain Way, and moving toward what he wanted; and he owns the house now, and is rebuilding it after the form of his mental image. And now, with still larger faith, he is going on to get greater things. It has been unto him according to his faith, and it is so with you and with all of us.

Gratitude

The illustrations given in the last chapter will have conveyed to the reader the fact that the first step toward getting rich is to convey the idea of your wants to the Formless Substance.

This is true, and you will see that in order to do so it becomes necessary to relate yourself to the Formless Intelligence in a harmonious way. Gratitude

To secure this harmonious relation is a matter of such primary and vital importance that I shall give some space to its discussion here, and give you instructions which, if you will follow them, will be certain to bring you into perfect unity of mind with God.

The whole process of mental adjustment and atonement can be summed up in one word, *gratitude*.

First, you believe that there is one Intelligent Substance, from which all things proceed; second, you believe that this Substance gives you everything you desire; and third, you relate yourself to It by a feeling of deep and profound gratitude.

Many people who order their lives rightly in all other ways are kept in poverty by their lack of gratitude. Having received one gift from God, they cut the wires which connect them with Him by failing to make acknowledgment.

It is easy to understand that the nearer we live to the source of wealth, the more wealth we shall receive; and it is easy also to understand that the soul that is always grateful lives in closer touch with God than the one which never looks to Him in thankful acknowledgment.

The more gratefully we fix our minds on the Supreme

when good things come to us, the more good things we will receive, and the more rapidly they will come; and the reason simply is that the mental attitude of gratitude draws the mind into closer touch with the source from which the blessings come.

If it is a new thought to you that gratitude brings your whole mind into closer harmony with the creative energies of the universe, consider it well, and you will see that it is true. The good things you already have come to you along the line of obedience to certain laws. Gratitude will lead your mind out along the ways by which things come; and it will keep you in close harmony with creative thought and prevent you from falling into competitive thought.

Gratitude alone can keep you looking toward the All, and prevent you from falling into the error of thinking of the supply as limited; and to do that would be fatal to your hopes.

There is a Law of Gratitude, and it is absolutely necessary that you should observe the law, if you are to get the results you seek.

The law of gratitude is the natural principle that action and reaction are always equal, and in opposite directions.

The grateful outreaching of your mind in thankful praise to the Supreme *is a liberation or expenditure of force; it cannot fail to reach that to which it is addressed, and the reaction is an instantaneous movement toward you.*

'Draw nigh unto God, and He will draw nigh unto you.' That is a statement of psychological truth.

And if your gratitude is strong and constant, the reaction in Formless Substance will be strong and continuous; the movement of the things you want will be always toward you.

Notice the grateful attitude that Jesus took; how He always seems to be saying, 'I thank Thee, Father, that Thou hearest me.' You cannot exercise much power without gratitude; for it is gratitude that keeps you connected with Power.

But the value of gratitude does not consist solely in getting you more blessings in the future. Without gratitude you cannot long keep from dissatisfied thought regarding things as they are.

The moment you permit your mind to dwell with dissatisfaction upon things as they are, you begin to lose ground. You fix attention upon the common, the ordinary, the poor, and the squalid and mean; and your mind takes the form of these things. Then you will transmit these forms or mental images to the Formless, and the common, the poor, the squalid, and mean will come to you.

To permit your mind to dwell upon the inferior is to become inferior and to surround yourself with inferior things.

On the other hand, to fix your attention on the best is to surround yourself with the best, and to become the best.

The Creative Power within us makes us into the image of that to which we give our attention.

We are Thinking Substance, and thinking substance always takes the form of that which it thinks about.

The grateful mind is constantly fixed upon the best; therefore, it tends to become the best; it takes the form or character of the best, and will receive the best.

Also, faith is born of gratitude. The grateful mind continually expects good things, and expectation becomes faith. The reaction of gratitude upon one's own mind produces faith; and every outgoing wave of grateful thanksgiving increases faith. He who has no feeling of gratitude cannot long retain a living faith and without a living faith you cannot get rich by the creative method, as we shall see in the following chapters.

It is necessary, then, to cultivate the habit of being grateful for every good thing that comes to you; and to give thanks continuously.

And because all things have contributed to your advancement, you should include all things in your gratitude.

Do not waste time thinking or talking about the shortcomings or wrong actions of plutocrats or trust magnates. Their organisation of the world has made your opportunity; all you get really comes to you because of them.

Do not rage against corrupt politicians; if it were not for politicians we should fall into anarchy, and your opportunity would be greatly lessened.

God has worked a long time and very patiently to bring us up to where we are in industry and government, and He is going right on with His work. There is not the least doubt that He will do away with plutocrats, trust magnates, captains of industry, and politicians as soon as they can be spared; but in the meantime, behold they are all very good. Remember that they are all helping to arrange the lines of transmission along which your riches will come to you, and be grateful to them all. This will elative method, as we shall see in the following chapters.

It is necessary, then, to cultivate the habit of being grateful for every good thing that comes to you; and to give thanks continuously.

And because all things have contributed to your advancement, you should include all things in your gratitude.

Do not waste time thinking or talking about the shortcomings or wrong actions of plutocrats or trust magnates. Their organisation of the world has made your opportunity; all you get really comes to you because of them.

Do not rage against corrupt politicians; if it were not for politicians we should fall into anarchy, and your opportunity would be greatly lessened.

God has worked a long time and very patiently to bring us up to where we are in industry and government, and He is going right on with His work. There is not the least doubt that He will do away with plutocrats, trust magnates, captains of industry, and politicians as soon as they can be spared; but in the meantime, behold they are all very good. Remember that they are all helping to arrange the lines of transmission along which your riches will come to you, and be grateful to them all. This will bring you into harmonious relations with the good in everything, and the good in everything will move toward you.

Acting in a Certain way

Thought is the creative power, or the impelling force which causes the creative power to act; thinking in a Certain Way will bring riches to you, but you must not rely upon thought alone, paying no attention to personal action. That is the rock upon which many otherwise scientific metaphysical thinkers meet shipwreck—the failure to connect thought with personal action.

We have not yet reached the stage of development, even supposing such a stage to be possible, in which man can create directly from Formless Substance without nature's processes or the work of human hands; man must not only think, but his personal action must supplement his thought.

By thought you can cause the gold in the hearts of the mountains to be impelled toward you; but it will not mine itself, refine itself, coin itself into double eagles, and come rolling along the roads seeking its way into your pocket.

Under the impelling power of the Supreme Spirit, men's affairs will be so ordered that someone will be led to mine the gold for you; other men's business transactions will be so directed that the gold will be brought toward you, and you must so arrange your own business affairs that you may be able to receive it when it comes to you. Your thought makes all things, animate and inanimate, work to bring you what you want; but your personal activity must be such that you can rightly receive what you want when it reaches you. You are not to take it as charity, nor to steal it; you must give every man more in use value than he gives you in cash value.

The scientific use of thought consists in forming a clear and distinct mental image of what you want; in holding fast to the purpose to get what you want; and in realizing with grateful faith that you *do* get what you want.

Do not try to 'project' your thought in any mysterious or occult way, with the idea of having it go out and do things for you; that is wasted effort, and will weaken your power to think with sanity.

The action of thought in getting rich is fully explained in the preceding chapters; your faith and purpose positively impress your vision upon Formless Substance, which has the same desire for more life that you have; and this vision, received from you, sets all the creative forces at work in and through their regular channels of action, but directed toward you.

It is not your part to guide or supervise the creative process; all you have to do with that is to retain your vision, stick to your purpose, and maintain your faith and gratitude.

But you must act in a Certain Way, so that you can appropriate what is yours when it comes to you; so that you can meet the things you have in your picture, and put them in their proper places as they arrive.

You can readily see the truth of this. When things reach you, they will be in the hands of other men, who will ask an equivalent for them.

And you can only get what is yours by giving the other man what is his.

Your pocketbook is not going to be transformed into a Fortunatus's purse, which shall be always full of money without effort on your part.

This is the crucial point in the science of getting rich; right here, where thought and personal action must be combined. There are very many people who, consciously or unconsciously, set the creative forces in action by the strength and persistence of their desires, but who remain poor because they do not provide for the reception of the thing they want when it comes.

By thought, the thing you want is brought to you; by action you receive it.

Whatever your action is to be, it is evident that you must act now. You cannot act in the past, and it is essential to the clearness of your mental vision that you dismiss the past from your mind. You cannot act in the future, for the future is not here yet. And you cannot tell how you will want to act in any

future contingency until that contingency has arrived.

Because you are not in the right business, or the right environment now, do not think that you must postpone action until you get into the right business or environment. And do not spend time in the present taking thought as to the best course in possible future emergencies; have faith in your ability to meet any emergency when it arrives.

If you act in the present with your mind on the future, your present action will be with a divided mind, and will not be effective.

Put your whole mind into present action.

Do not give your creative impulse to Original Substance, and then sit down and wait for results; if you do, you will never get them. Act now. There is never any time but now, and there never will be any time but now. If you are ever to begin to make ready for the reception of what you want, you must begin now.

And your action, whatever it is, must most likely be in your present business or employment, and must be upon the persons and things in your present environment.

You cannot act where you are not; you cannot act where you have been, and you cannot act where you are going to be; you can act only where you are.

Do not bother as to whether yesterday's work was well done or ill done; do to-day's work well.

Do not try to do to-morrow's work now; there will be plenty of time to do that when you get to it.

Do not try, by occult or mystical means, to act on people or things that are out of your reach.

Do not wait for a change of environment before you act;

get a change of environment by action.

You can so act upon the environment in which you are now, as to cause yourself to be transferred to a better environment.

Hold with faith and purpose the vision of yourself in the better environment, but act upon your present environment with all your heart, and with all your strength, and with all your mind.

Do not spend any time in day dreaming or castle building; hold to the one vision of what you want, and act now.

Do not cast about seeking some new thing to do, or some strange, unusual, or remarkable action to perform as a first step toward getting rich. It is probable that your actions, at least for some time to come, will be those you have been performing for some time past; but you are to begin now to perform these actions in the Certain Way, which will surely make you rich.

If you are engaged in some business, and feel that it is not the right one for you, do not wait until you get into the right business before you begin to act.

Do not feel discouraged, or sit down and lament because you are misplaced. No man was ever so misplaced but that he could find the right place, and no man ever became so involved in the wrong business but that he could get into the right business.

Hold the vision of yourself in the right business, with the purpose to get into it, and the faith that you will get into it, and are getting into it; but act in your present business. Use your present business as the means of getting a better one, and use your present environment as the means of getting into a better one. Your vision of the right business, if held with faith and purpose, will cause the Supreme to move the right business toward you; and your action, if performed in

the Certain Way, will cause you to move toward the business.

If you are an employee, or wage earner, and feel that you must change places in order to get what you want, do not 'project' your thought into space and rely upon it to get you another job. It will probably fail to do so.

Hold the vision of yourself in the job you want, while you act with faith and purpose on the job you have, and you will certainly get the job you want.

Your vision and faith will set the creative force in motion to bring it toward you, and your action will cause the forces in your own environment to move you toward the place you want. In closing this chapter, we will add another statement to our syllabus:

There is a thinking stuff from which all things are made, and which, in its original state, permeates, penetrates, and fills the interspaces of the universe.

A thought, in this substance, produces the thing that is imaged by the thought.

Man can form things in his thought, and, by impressing his thoughts upon formless substance, can cause the thing he thinks about to be created.

In order to do this, man must pass from the competitive to the creative mind; he must form a clear mental picture of the things he wants, and hold this picture in his thoughts with the fixed Purpose to get what he wants, and the unwavering Faith that he does get what he wants, closing his mind to all that may tend to shake his purpose, dim his vision, or quench his faith.

That he may receive what he wants when it comes, man must act Now upon the people and things in his present environment.

The Impression of Increase

Whether you change your vocation or not, your actions for the present must be those pertaining to the business in which you are now engaged.

You can get into the business you want by making constructive use of the business you are already established in; by doing your daily work in a Certain Way. The Impression of Increase

And in so far as your business consists in dealing with other men, whether personally or by letter, the key-thought of all your efforts must be to convey to their minds the impression of increase.

Increase is what all men and all women are seeking; it is the urge of the Formless Intelligence within them, seeking fuller expression.

The desire for increase is inherent in all nature; it is the fundamental impulse of the universe. All human activities are based on the desire -for increase; people are seeking more food, more clothes, better shelter, more luxury, more beauty, more knowledge, more pleasure—increase in something, more life.

Every living thing is under this necessity for continuous advancement; where increase of life ceases, dissolution and death set in at once.

Man instinctively knows this, and hence he is forever seeking more. This law of perpetual increase is set forth by Jesus in the parable of the talents; only those who gain more retain any; from him who hath not shall be taken away even that which he hath.

The normal desire for increased wealth is not an evil or a reprehensible thing; it is simply the desire for more abundant life; it is aspiration.

And because it is the deepest instinct of their natures, all men and women are attracted to him who can give them more of the means of life.

In following the Certain Way as described in the foregoing pages, you are getting continuous increase for yourself, and you are giving it to all with whom you deal.

Be sure of this, and convey assurance of the fact to every man, woman, and child with whom you come in contact. No matter how small the transaction, even if it be only the selling of a stick of candy to a little child, put into it the thought of increase, and make sure that the customer is impressed with the thought.

Convey the impression of advancement with everything you do, so that all people shall receive the impression that you are an Advancing Man, and that you advance all who deal with you. Even to the people whom you meet in a social way, without any thought of business, and to whom you do not try to sell anything, give the thought of increase.

You can convey this impression by holding the unshakable faith that you, yourself, are in the Way of Increase; and by letting this faith inspire, fill, and permeate every action.

Do everything that you do in the firm conviction that you are an advancing personality, and that you are giving advancement to everybody.

Feel that you are getting rich, and that in so doing you are making others rich, and conferring benefits on all.

Do not boast or brag of your success, or talk about it unnecessarily; true faith is never boastful.

Wherever you find a boastful person, you find one who is secretly doubtful and afraid. Simply feel the faith, and let it work out in every transaction; let every act and tone and look express the quiet assurance that you are getting rich; that you are already rich. Words will not be necessary to communicate this feeling to others; they will feel the sense of increase when in your presence, and will be attracted to you again.

You must so impress others that they will feel that in associating with you they will get increase for themselves. See that you give them a use value greater than the cash value you are taking from them.

Take an honest pride in doing this, and let everybody know it; and you will have no lack of customers. People will go where they are given increase; and the Supreme, which desires increase in all, and which knows all, will move toward you men and women who have never heard of you. Your business will increase rapidly, and you will be surprised at the unexpected benefits which will come to you. You will be able from day to day to make larger combinations, secure greater advantages, and to go on into a more congenial vocation if you desire to do so.

But in doing all this, you must never lose sight of your vision of what you want, or your faith and purpose to get what you want.

Let me here give you another word of caution in regard to motives.

Beware of the insidious temptation to seek for power over other men.

Nothing is so pleasant to the unformed or partially developed mind as the exercise of power or dominion over others. The desire to rule for selfish gratification has been the curse of the world. For countless ages kings and lords have drenched the earth with blood in their battles to extend their dominions; this not to seek more life for all, but to get more power for themselves.

To-day, the main motive in the business and industrial world is the same; men marshal their armies of dollars, and lay waste the lives and hearts of millions in the same mad scramble for power over others. Commercial kings, like political kings, are inspired by the lust for power.

Jesus saw in this desire for mastery the moving impulse of that evil world He sought to overthrow. Read the twenty-third chapter of Matthew, and see how He pictures the lust of the Pharisees to be called 'Master,' to sit in the high places, to domineer over others, and to lay burdens on the backs of the less fortunate; and note how He compares this lust for dominion with the brotherly seeking for the Common Good to which He calls His disciples.

Look out for the temptation to seek for authority, to become a 'master,' to be considered as one who is above the common herd, to impress others by lavish display, and so on.

The mind that seeks for mastery over others is the competitive mind; and the competitive mind is not the creative one. In order to master your environment and your destiny, it is not at all necessary that you should rule over your fellow men; and indeed, when you fall into the world's struggle for the high places, you begin to be conquered by fate and environment, and your getting rich becomes a matter of chance and speculation.

Beware of the competitive mind! No better statement of the principle of creative action can be formulated than the favourite declaration of the late 'Golden Rule' Jones of Toledo: 'What I want for myself, I want for everybody.'

SECTION THREE

THE ART OF MONEY GETTING
by PT Barnum

'Money is, in some respects, like fire. It is a very excellent
servant, but a terrible master.'

Don't Mistake Your Vocation

The safest plan, and the one most sure of success for the young man starting in life, is to select the vocation which is most congenial to his tastes. Parents and guardians are often quite too negligent in regard to this. It very common for a father to say, for example: 'I have five boys. I will make Billy a clergyman; John a lawyer; Tom a doctor, and Dick a farmer.' He then goes into town and looks about to see what he will do with Sammy. He returns home and says 'Sammy, I see watch-making is a nice genteel business; I think I will make you a goldsmith.' He does this, regardless of Sam's natural inclinations, or genius. Don't mistake your vocation.

We are all, no doubt, born for a wise purpose. There is as much diversity in our brains as in our countenances. Some are born natural mechanics, while some have great aversion to machinery. Let a dozen boys of ten years get together, and you will soon observe two or three are 'whittling' out some ingenious device; working with locks or complicated machinery. When they were but five years old, their father could find no toy to please them like a puzzle. They are natural mechanics; but the other eight or nine boys have different aptitudes. I belong to the latter class; I never had the slightest love for mechanism; on the contrary, I have a sort of abhorrence for complicated machinery. I never had ingenuity enough to whittle a cider tap so it would not leak. I never could make a pen that I could write with, or understand the principle of a steam engine. If a man was to take such a boy as I was, and attempt to make a watchmaker of him, the boy might, after an apprenticeship of five or seven years, be able to take apart and put together a watch; but all through life he would be working up hill and seizing every excuse for leaving his work and idling away his time. Watchmaking is repulsive to him.

Unless a man enters upon the vocation intended for him by nature, and best suited to his peculiar genius, he cannot succeed. I am glad to believe that the majority of persons do find their right vocation. Yet we see many who have mistaken their calling, from the blacksmith up (or down) to the clergyman. You will see, for instance, that extraordinary linguist the 'learned blacksmith,' who ought to have been a teacher of languages; and you may have seen lawyers, doctors and clergymen who were better fitted by nature for the anvil or the lap stone.

⬭ ⬭ ⬭

Select the Right Location

After securing the right vocation, you must be careful to select the proper location. You may have been cut out for a hotel keeper, and they say it requires a genius to 'know how to keep a hotel.' You might conduct a hotel like clock-work, and provide satisfactorily for five hundred guests every day; yet, if you should locate your house in a small village where there is no railroad communication or public travel, the location would be your ruin. It is equally important that you do not commence business where there are already enough to meet all demands in the same occupation. I remember a case which illustrates this subject. When I was in London in 1858, I was passing down Holborn with an English friend and came to the 'penny shows.' They had immense cartoons outside, portraying the wonderful curiosities to be seen 'all for a penny.' Being a little in the 'show line' myself, I said 'let us go in here.' We soon found ourselves in the presence of the illustrious showman, and he proved to be the sharpest man in that line I had ever met. He told us some extraordinary stories in reference to his bearded ladies, his Albinos, and his Armadillos, which we could hardly believe, but thought it 'better to believe it than look after the proof'.' He finally begged to call our attention to some wax statuary, and showed us a lot of the dirtiest and filthiest wax figures imaginable. They looked as if they had not seen water since the Deluge.

'What is there so wonderful about your statuary?' I asked.

'I beg you not to speak so satirically,' he replied, 'Sir, these are not Madam Tussaud's wax figures, all covered with gilt and tinsel and imitation diamonds, and copied from engravings and photographs. Mine, sir, were taken from life. Whenever you look upon one of those figures, you may consider that you are looking upon the living individual.'

Glancing casually at them, I saw one labelled 'Henry VIII,' and feeling a little curious upon seeing that it looked like Calvin Edson, the living skeleton, I said: 'Do you call that 'Henry the Eighth?'' He replied, 'Certainly; sir; it was taken from life at Hampton Court, by special order of his majesty; on such a day.'

He would have given the hour of the day if I had resisted; I said, 'Everybody knows that 'Henry VIII.' was a great stout old king, and that figure is lean and lank; what do you say to that?'

'Why,' he replied, 'you would be lean and lank yourself if you sat there as long as he has.'

There was no resisting such arguments. I said to my English friend, 'Let us go out; do not tell him who I am; I show the white feather; he beats me.'

He followed us to the door, and seeing the rabble in the street, he called out, 'ladies and gentlemen, I beg to draw your attention to the respectable character of my visitors,' pointing to us as we walked away. I called upon him a couple of days afterwards; told him who I was, and said:

'My friend, you are an excellent showman, but you have selected a bad location.'

He replied, 'This is true, sir; I feel that all my talents are thrown away; but what can I do?'

'You can go to America,' I replied. 'You can give full play to your faculties over there; you will find plenty of elbowroom in America; I will engage you for two years; after that you will be able to go on your own account.'

He accepted my offer and remained two years in my New York Museum. He then went to New Orleans and carried on a traveling show business during the summer. To-day he is worth sixty thousand dollars, simply because he selected the right vocation and also secured the proper location. The old proverb says, 'Three removes are as bad as a fire,' but when a man is in the fire, it matters but little how soon or how often he removes.

Avoid Debt

Young men starting in life should avoid running into debt. There is scarcely anything that drags a person down like debt. It is a slavish position to get in, yet we find many a young man, hardly out of his 'teens,' running in debt. He meets a chum and says, 'Look at this: I have got trusted for a new suit of clothes.' He seems to look upon the clothes as so much given to him; well, it frequently is so, but, if he succeeds in paying and then gets trusted again, he is adopting a habit which will keep him in poverty through life. Debt robs a man of his self-respect, and makes him almost despise himself.

Grunting and groaning and working for what he has eaten up or worn out, and now when he is called upon to pay up, he has nothing to show for his money; this is properly termed 'working for a dead horse.' I do not speak of merchants buying and selling on credit, or of those who buy on credit in order to turn the purchase to a profit. The old Quaker said to his farmer son, 'John, never get trusted; but if thee gets trusted for anything, let it be for 'manure,' because that will help thee pay it back again.'

Mr Beecher advised young men to get in debt if they could to a small amount in the purchase of land, in the country districts. 'If a young man,' he says, 'will only get in debt for some land and then get married, these two things will keep him straight, or nothing will.' This may be safe to a limited extent, but getting in debt for what you eat and drink and wear is to be avoided. Some families have a foolish habit of getting credit at 'the stores,' and thus frequently purchase many things which might have been dispensed with.

It is all very well to say; 'I have got trusted for sixty days, and if I don't have the money the creditor will think nothing about it.' There is no class of people in the world, who have such good memories as creditors. When the sixty days run out, you will have to pay. If you do not pay, you will break your promise, and probably resort to a falsehood. You may make some excuse or get in debt elsewhere to pay it, but that only involves you the deeper.

A good-looking, lazy young fellow, was the apprentice boy, Horatio. His employer said, 'Horatio, did you ever see a snail?' 'I—think—I—have,' he drawled out. 'You must have met him then, for I am sure you never overtook one,' said the 'boss.' Your creditor will meet you or overtake you and say, 'Now, my young friend, you agreed to pay me; you have not done it, you must give me your note.' You give the note on interest and it commences working against you; 'it is a dead horse.' The creditor goes to bed at night and wakes up in the morning better off than when he retired to bed, because his interest has increased during the night, but you grow poorer while you are sleeping, for the interest is accumulating against you.

Money is in some respects like fire; it is a very excellent servant but a terrible master. When you have it mastering you; when interest is constantly piling up against you, it will keep you down in the worst kind of slavery. But let money work for you, and you have the most devoted servant in the world. It is no 'eye-servant.' There is nothing animate or inanimate that will work so faithfully as money when placed at interest, well secured. It works night and day, and in wet or dry weather.

I was born in the blue-law State of Connecticut, where the old Puritans had laws so rigid that it was said, 'they fined a man for kissing his wife on Sunday.' Yet these rich old Puritans would have thousands of dollars at interest, and on Saturday night would be worth a certain amount; on Sunday they would go to church and perform all the duties of a Christian. On waking up on Monday morning, they would find themselves considerably richer than the Saturday night previous, simply because their money placed at interest had worked faithfully for them all day Sunday, according to law!

Do not let it work against you; if you do there is no chance for success in life so far as money is concerned. John Randolph, the eccentric Virginian, once exclaimed in Congress, 'Mr Speaker, I have discovered the philosopher's stone: pay as you go.' This is, indeed, nearer to the philosopher's stone than any alchemist has ever yet arrived.

Persevere

When a man is in the right path, he must persevere. I speak of this because there are some persons who are 'born tired;' naturally lazy and possessing no self-reliance and no perseverance. But they can cultivate these qualities, as Davy Crockett said:

'This thing remember, when I am dead: Be sure you are right, then go ahead.'

It is this go-aheaditiveness, this determination not to let the 'horrors' or the 'blues' take possession of you, so as to make you relax your energies in the struggle for independence, which you must cultivate.

How many have almost reached the goal of their ambition, but, losing faith in themselves, have relaxed their energies, and the golden prize has been lost forever.

It is, no doubt, often true, as Shakespeare says:

'There is a tide in the affairs of men, Which, taken at the flood, leads on to fortune.'

If you hesitate, some bolder hand will stretch out before you and get the prize. Remember the proverb of Solomon: 'He becometh poor that dealeth with a slack hand; but the hand of the diligent maketh rich.'

Perseverance is sometimes but another word for self-reliance. Many persons naturally look on the dark side of life, and borrow trouble. They are born so. Then they ask for advice, and they will be governed by one wind and blown by another, and cannot rely upon themselves. Until you can get so that you can rely upon yourself, you need not expect to succeed.

I have known men, personally, who have met with pecuniary reverses, and absolutely committed suicide, because they thought they could never overcome their misfortune. But I have known others who have met more serious financial difficulties, and have bridged them over by simple perseverance, aided by a firm belief that they were doing justly, and that Providence would 'overcome evil with good.' You will see this illustrated in any sphere of life.

Take two generals; both understand military tactics, both educated at West Point, if you please, both equally gifted; yet one, having this principle of perseverance, and the other lacking it, the former will succeed in his profession, while the latter will fail. One may hear the cry, 'the enemy are coming, and they have got cannon.'

'Got cannon?' says the hesitating general.

'Yes.'

'Then halt every man.'

He wants time to reflect; his hesitation is his ruin; the enemy passes unmolested, or overwhelms him; while on the other hand, the general of pluck, perseverance and self-reliance, goes into battle with a will, and, amid the clash of arms, the booming of cannon, the shrieks of the wounded, and the moans of the dying, you will see this man persevering, going on, cutting and slashing his way through with unwavering determination, inspiring his soldiers to deeds of fortitude, valour, and triumph.

Whatever you do, do it with all Your Might

Work at it, if necessary, early and late, in season and out of season, not leaving a stone unturned, and never deferring for a single hour that which can be done just as well now. The old proverb is full of truth and meaning, 'Whatever is worth doing at all, is worth doing well.' Many a man acquires a fortune by doing his business thoroughly, while his neighbour remains poor for life, because he only half does it. Ambition, energy, industry, perseverance, are indispensable requisites for success in business.

Fortune always favours the brave, and never helps a man who does not help himself. It won't do to spend your time like Mr Micawber, in waiting for something to 'turn up.' To such men one of two things usually 'turns up:' the poorhouse or the jail; for idleness breeds bad habits, and clothes a man in rags. The poor spendthrift vagabond says to a rich man:

'I have discovered there is enough money in the world for all of us, if it was equally divided; this must be done, and we shall all be happy together.'

'But,' was the response, 'if everybody was like you, it would be spent in two months, and what would you do then?'

'Oh! divide again; keep dividing, of course!'

I was recently reading in a London paper an account of a like philosophic pauper who was kicked out of a cheap boarding-house because he could not pay his bill, but he had a roll of papers sticking out of his coat pocket, which, upon examination, proved to be his plan for paying off the national debt of England without the aid of a penny. People have got to do as Cromwell said: 'not only trust in Providence, but keep the powder dry.' Do your part of the work, or you cannot succeed. Mahomet, one night, while encamping in the desert, overheard one of his fatigued followers remark: 'I will lose my camel, and trust it to God!' 'No, no, not so,' said the prophet, 'tie thy camel, and trust it to God!' Do all you can for yourselves, and then trust to Providence, or luck, or whatever you please to call it, for the rest.

Depend Upon Your own Personal Exertions

The eye of the employer is often worth more than the hands of a dozen employees. In the nature of things, an agent cannot be so faithful to his employer as to himself. Many who are employers will call to mind instances where the best employees have overlooked important points which could not have escaped their own observation as a proprietor. No man has a right to expect to succeed in life unless he understands his business, and nobody can understand his business thoroughly unless he learns it by personal application and experience.

A man may be a manufacturer: he has got to learn the many details of his business personally; he will learn something every day, and he will find he will make mistakes nearly every day. And these very mistakes are helps to him in the way of experiences if he but heeds them. He will be like the Yankee tin-peddler, who, having been cheated as to quality in the purchase of his merchandise, said: 'All right, there's a little information to be gained every day; I will never be cheated in that way again.' Thus a man buys his experience, and it is the best kind if not purchased at too dear a rate.

I hold that every man should, like Cuvier, the French naturalist, thoroughly know his business. So proficient was he in the study of natural history, that you might bring to him the bone, or even a section of a bone of an animal which he had never seen described, and, reasoning from analogy, he would be able to draw a picture of the object from which the bone had been taken. On one occasion his students attempted to deceive him. They rolled one of their number in a cow skin and put him under the professor's table as a new specimen. When the philosopher came into the room, some of the students asked him what animal it was. Suddenly the animal said 'I am the devil and I am going to eat you.' It was but natural that Cuvier should desire to classify this creature, and examining it intently, he said:

'Divided hoof; graminivorous! It cannot be done.'

He knew that an animal with a split hoof must live upon grass and grain, or other kind of vegetation, and would not be inclined to eat flesh, dead or alive, so he considered himself perfectly safe. The possession of a perfect knowledge of your business is an absolute necessity in order to insure success.

Among the maxims of the elder Rothschild was one, all apparent paradox: 'Be cautious and bold.' This seems to be a contradiction in terms, but it is not, and there is great wisdom in the maxim. It is, in fact, a condensed statement of what I have already said. It is to say; 'you must exercise your caution in laying your plans, but be bold in carrying them out.' A man who is all caution, will never dare to take hold and be successful; and a man who is all boldness, is merely reckless, and must eventually fail. A man may go on 'change' and make fifty, or one hundred thousand dollars in speculating in stocks, at a single operation. But if he has simple boldness without caution, it is mere chance, and what he gains to-day he will lose to-morrow. You must have both the caution and the boldness, to insure success.

The Rothschilds have another maxim: 'Never have anything to do with an unlucky man or place.' That is to say, never have anything to do with a man or place which never succeeds, because, although a man may appear to be honest and intelligent, yet if he tries this or that thing and always fails, it is on account of some fault or infirmity that you may not be able to discover but nevertheless which must exist.

There is no such thing in the world as luck. There never was a man who could go out in the morning and find a purse full of gold in the street to-day, and another to-morrow, and so on, day after day: He may do so once in his life; but so far as mere luck is concerned, he is as liable to lose it as to find it. 'Like causes produce like effects.' If a man adopts the proper methods to be successful, 'luck' will not prevent him. If he does not succeed, there are reasons for it, although, perhaps, he may not be able to see them.

Use the Best Tools

Men in engaging employees should be careful to get the best. Understand, you cannot have too good tools to work with, and there is no tool you should be so particular about as living tools. If you get a good one, it is better to keep him, than keep changing. He learns something every day; and you are benefited by the experience he acquires. He is worth more to you this year than last, and he is the last man to part with, provided his habits are good, and he continues faithful. If, as he gets more valuable, he demands an exorbitant increase of salary; on the supposition that you can't do without him, let him go. Whenever I have such an employee, I always discharge him; first, to convince him that his place may be supplied, and second, because he is good for nothing if he thinks he is invaluable and cannot be spared.

But I would keep him, if possible, in order to profit from the result of his experience. An important element in an employee is the brain. You can see bills up, 'Hands Wanted,'

but 'hands' are not worth a great deal without 'heads.'
Mr Beecher illustrates this, in this wise:

An employee offers his services by saving, 'I have a pair of
hands and one of my fingers thinks.' 'That is very good,' says
the employer. Another man comes along, and says 'he has two
fingers that think.' 'Ah! that is better.' But a third calls in and
says that 'all his fingers and thumbs think.' That is better still.
Finally another steps in and says, 'I have a brain that thinks; I
think all over; I am a thinking as well as a working man!' 'You
are the man I want,' says the delighted employer.

Those men who have brains and experience are therefore
the most valuable and not to be readily parted with; it is better
for them, as well as yourself, to keep them, at reasonable
advances in their salaries from time to time.

Don't get Above Your Business

Young men after they get through their business training, or apprenticeship, instead of pursuing their avocation and rising in their business, will often lie about doing nothing. They say; 'I have learned my business, but I am not going to be a hireling; what is the object of learning my trade or profession, unless I establish myself?"

'You have ' capital to start with?'

'No, but I am going to have it.'

'How are you going to get it?'

'I will tell you confidentially; I have a wealthy old aunt, and she will die pretty soon; but if she does not, I expect to find some rich old man who will lend me a few thousands to give me a start. If I only get the money to start with I will do well.'

There is no greater mistake than when a young man believes he will succeed with borrowed money. Why? Because every man's experience coincides with that of Mr Astor, who said, 'it was more difficult for him to accumulate his first thousand dollars, than all the succeeding millions that made up his colossal fortune.' Money is good for nothing unless you know the value of it by experience. Give a boy twenty thousand dollars and put him in business, and the chances are that he will lose every dollar of it before he is a year older. Like buying a ticket in the lottery; and drawing a prize, it is 'easy come, easy go.' He does not know the value of it; nothing is worth anything, unless it costs effort. Without self-denial and economy; patience and perseverance, and commencing with capital which you have not earned, you are not sure to succeed in accumulating. Young men, instead of 'waiting for dead men's shoes,' should be up and doing, for there is no class of persons who are so unaccommodating in regard to dying as these rich old people, and it is fortunate for the expectant heirs that it is so.

Nine out of ten of the rich men of our country to-day, started out in life as poor boys, with determined wills, industry, perseverance, economy and good habits. They went on gradually, made their own money and saved it; and this is the best way to acquire a fortune. Stephen Girard started life as a poor cabin boy, and died worth nine million dollars. A.T. Stewart was a poor Irish boy; and he paid taxes on a million and a half dollars of income, per year. John Jacob Astor was a poor farmer boy, and died worth twenty million. Cornelius Vanderbilt began life rowing a boat from Staten Island to New York; he presented our government with a steamship worth a million of dollars, and died worth fifty million.

'There is no royal road to learning,' says the proverb, and I may say it is equally true, 'there is no royal road to wealth.' But I think there is a royal road to both. The road to learning is a royal one; the road that enables the student to expand his intellect and add every day to his stock of knowledge, until, in the pleasant process of intellectual growth, he is able to solve the most profound problems, to count the stars, to analyse every atom of the globe, and to measure the firmament this is a regal highway, and it is the only road worth traveling.

So in regard to wealth. Go on in confidence, study the rules, and above all things, study human nature; for 'the proper study of mankind is man,' and you will find that while expanding the intellect and the muscles, your enlarged experience will enable you every day to accumulate more and more principal, which will increase itself by interest and otherwise, until you arrive at a state of independence. You will find, as a general thing, that the poor boys get rich and the rich boys get poor.

For instance, a rich man at his decease, leaves a large estate to his family. His eldest sons, who have helped him earn his fortune, known by experience the value of money; and they take their inheritance and add to it. The separate portions of the young children are placed at interest, and the little fellows are patted on the head, and told a dozen times a day, 'you are rich; you will never have to work, you can always have whatever you wish, for you were born with a golden spoon in your mouth.' The young heir soon finds out what that means; he has the finest dresses and playthings; he is crammed with sugar candies and almost 'killed with kindness,' and he passes from school to school, petted and flattered.

He becomes arrogant and self-conceited, abuses his teachers, and carries everything with a high hand. He knows nothing of the real value of money, having never earned any;

but he knows all about the 'golden spoon' business. At college, he invites his poor fellow-students to his room, where he 'wines and dines' them. He is cajoled and caressed, and called a glorious good follow, because he is so lavish of his money. He gives his game suppers, drives his fast horses, invites his chums to fetes and parties, determined to have lots of 'good times.' He spends the night in frolics and debauchery, and leads off his companions with the familiar song, 'we won't go home till morning.' He gets them to join him in pulling down signs, taking gates from their hinges and throwing them into back yards and horse-ponds. If the police arrest them, he knocks them down, is taken to the lockup, and joyfully foots the bills.

'Ah! my boys,' he cries, 'what is the use of being rich, if you can't enjoy yourself?'

He might more truly say, 'if you can't make a fool of yourself;' but he is 'fast,' hates slow things, and doesn't 'see it.' Young men loaded down with other people's money are almost sure to lose all they inherit, and they acquire all sorts of bad habits which, in the majority of cases, ruin them in health, purse and character. In this country, one generation follows another, and the poor of to-day are rich in the next generation, or the third. Their experience leads them on, and they become rich, and they leave vast riches to their young children. These children, having been reared in luxury, are inexperienced and get poor; and after long experience another generation comes on and gathers up riches again in turn. And thus 'history repeats itself,' and happy is he who by listening to the experience of others avoids the rocks and shoals on which so many have been wrecked.

'In England, the business makes the man.' If a man in that

country is a mechanic or working-man, he is not recognized as a gentleman. On the occasion of my first appearance before Queen Victoria, the Duke of Wellington asked me what sphere in life General Tom Thumb's parents were in.

'His father is a carpenter,' I replied.

'Oh! I had heard he was a gentleman,' was the response of His Grace.

In this Republican country, the man makes the business. No matter whether he is a blacksmith, a shoemaker, a farmer, banker or lawyer, so long as his business is legitimate, he may be a gentleman. So any 'legitimate' business is a double blessing it helps the man engaged in it, and also helps others. The Farmer supports his own family, but he also benefits the merchant or mechanic who needs the products of his farm. The tailor not only makes a living by his trade, but he also benefits the farmer, the clergyman and others who cannot make their own clothing. But all these classes often may be gentlemen.

The great ambition should be to excel all others engaged in the same occupation.

The college-student who was about graduating, said to an old lawyer:

'I have not yet decided which profession I will follow. Is your profession full?'

'The basement is much crowded, but there is plenty of room up-stairs,' was the witty and truthful reply.

No profession, trade, or calling, is overcrowded in the upper story. Wherever you find the most honest and intelligent merchant or banker, or the best lawyer, the best doctor, the best clergyman, the best shoemaker, carpenter, or anything else, that man is most sought for, and has always enough to do. As a nation, Americans are too superficial—they are striving to get rich quickly, and do not generally do their business as substantially and thoroughly as they should, but whoever excels all others in his own line, if his habits are good and his integrity undoubted, cannot fail to secure abundant patronage, and the wealth that naturally follows. Let your motto then always be 'Excelsior,' for by living up to it there is no such word as fail.

Be Systematic

Men should be systematic in their business. A person who does business by rule, having a time and place for everything, doing his work promptly, will accomplish twice as much and with half the trouble of him who does it carelessly and slipshod. By introducing system into all your transactions, doing one thing at a time, always meeting appointments with punctuality, you find leisure for pastime and recreation; whereas the man who only half does one thing, and then turns to something else, and half does that, will have his business at loose ends, and will never know when his day's work is done, for it never will be done. Of course, there is a limit to all these rules. We must try to preserve the happy medium, for there is such a thing as being too systematic. There are men and women, for instance, who put away things so carefully that they can never find them again. It is too much like the 'red tape' formality at Washington, and Mr Dickens' 'Circumlocution Office,'—all theory and no result.

When the 'Astor House' was first started in New York city, it was undoubtedly the best hotel in the country. The proprietors had learned a good deal in Europe regarding hotels, and the landlords were proud of the rigid system which pervaded every department of their great establishment. When twelve o'clock at night had arrived, and there were a number of guests around, one of the proprietors would say, 'Touch that bell, John;' and in two minutes sixty servants, with a water-bucket in each hand, would present themselves in the hall. 'This,' said the landlord, addressing his guests, 'is our fire-bell; it will show you we are quite safe here; we do everything systematically.'

This was before the Croton water was introduced into the city. But they sometimes carried their system too far. On one occasion, when the hotel was thronged with guests, one of the waiters was suddenly indisposed, and although there were fifty waiters in the hotel, the landlord thought he must have his full complement, or his 'system' would be interfered with. Just before dinner-time, he rushed down stairs and said, 'There must be another waiter, I am one waiter short, what can I do?' He happened to see 'Boots,' the Irishman. 'Pat,' said he, 'wash your hands and face; take that white apron and come into the dining-room in five minutes.' Presently Pat appeared as required, and the proprietor said: 'Now Pat, you must stand behind these two chairs, and wait on the gentlemen who will occupy them; did you ever act as a waiter?'

'I know all about it, sure, but I never did it.'

Like the Irish pilot, on one occasion when the captain, thinking he was considerably out of his course, asked, 'Are you certain you understand what you are doing?'

Pat replied, 'Sure and I know every rock in the channel.'

That moment, 'bang' thumped the vessel against a rock.

'Ah! be-jabers, and that is one of 'em,' continued the pilot. But to return to the dining-room. 'Pat,' said the landlord, 'here we do everything systematically. You must first give the gentlemen each a plate of soup, and when they finish that, ask them what they will have next.'

Pat replied, 'Ah! an' I understand perfectly the virtues of system.'

Very soon in came the guests. The plates of soup were placed before them. One of Pat's two gentlemen ate his soup; the other did not care for it. He said: 'Waiter, take this plate away and bring me some fish.' Pat looked at the untasted plate of soup, and remembering the instructions of the landlord in regard to 'system,' replied: 'Not till ye have ate yer supe!' of course that was carrying 'system' entirely too far.

Beware of 'Outside Operations'

Beware of 'Outside Operations' We sometimes see men who have obtained fortunes, suddenly become poor. In many cases, this arises from intemperance, and often from gaming, and other bad habits. Frequently it occurs because a man has been engaged in 'outside operations,' of some sort. When he gets rich in his legitimate business, he is told of a grand speculation where he can make a score of thousands. He is constantly flattered by his friends, who tell him that he is born lucky, that everything he touches turns into gold. Now if he forgets that his economical habits, his rectitude of conduct and a personal attention to a business which he understood, caused his success in life, he will listen to the siren voices. He says:

'I will put in twenty thousand dollars. I have been lucky, and my good luck will soon bring me back sixty thousand dollars.'

A few days elapse and it is discovered he must put in ten thousand dollars more: soon after he is told 'it is all right,' but certain matters not foreseen, require an advance of twenty thousand dollars more, which will bring him a rich harvest; but before the time comes around to realize, the bubble bursts, he loses all he is possessed of, and then he learns what he ought to have known at the first, that however successful a man may be in his own business, if he turns from that and engages ill a business which he don't understand, he is like Samson when shorn of his locks his strength has departed, and he becomes like other men.

If a man has plenty of money, he ought to invest something in everything that appears to promise success, and that will probably benefit mankind; but let the sums thus invested be moderate in amount, and never let a man foolishly jeopardise a fortune that he has earned in a legitimate way, by investing it in things in which he has had no experience.

Don't Endorse
Without Security

I hold that no man ought ever to endorse a note or become security, for any man, be it his father or brother, to a greater extent than he can afford to lose and care nothing about, without taking good security. Here is a man that is worth twenty thousand dollars; he is doing a thriving manufacturing or mercantile trade; you are retired and living on your money; he comes to you and says:

'You are aware that I am worth twenty thousand dollars, and don't owe a dollar; if I had five thousand dollars in cash, I could purchase a particular lot of goods and double my money in a couple of months; will you endorse my note for that amount?'

You reflect that he is worth twenty thousand dollars, and you incur no risk by endorsing his note; you like to accommodate him, and you lend your name without taking the precaution of getting security. Shortly after, he shows you the note with your endorsement cancelled, and tells you, probably truly, 'that he made the profit that he expected by the operation,' you reflect that you have done a good action, and the thought makes you feel happy. By and by, the same thing occurs again and you do it again; you have already fixed the impression in your mind that it is perfectly safe to indorse his notes without security.

But the trouble is, this man is getting money too easily. He has only to take your note to the bank, get it discounted and take the cash. He gets money for the time being without effort; without inconvenience to himself. Now mark the result. He sees a chance for speculation outside of his business. A temporary investment of only $10,000 is required. It is sure to come back before a note at the bank would be due. He places a note for that amount before you. You sign it almost mechanically. Being firmly convinced that your friend is responsible and trustworthy; you indorse his notes as a 'matter of course.'

Unfortunately, the speculation does not come to a head quite so soon as was expected, and another $10,000 note must be discounted to take up the last one when due. Before this note matures the speculation has proved an utter failure and all the money is lost. Does the loser tell his friend, the endorser, that he has lost half of his fortune? Not at all. He doesn't even mention that he has speculated at all. But he has got excited; the spirit of speculation has seized him; he sees others making large sums in this way (we seldom hear of the losers), and, like other speculators, he 'looks for his money where he loses it.' He tries again. endorsing notes has become chronic with you, and at every loss he gets your signature for whatever amount he wants. Finally, you discover your friend has lost all of his property and all of yours. You are overwhelmed with astonishment and grief, and you say 'it is a hard thing; my friend here has ruined me,' but, you should add, 'I have also ruined him.' If you had said in the first place, 'I will accommodate you, but I never indorse without taking ample security,' he could not have gone beyond the length of his tether, and he would never have been tempted away from his legitimate business. It is a very dangerous thing, therefore, at any time, to let people get possession of money too easily; it tempts them to hazardous speculations, if nothing more. Solomon truly said 'he that hateth suretyship is sure.'

So with the young man starting in business; let him understand the value of money by earning it. When he does understand its value, then grease the wheels a little in helping him to start business, but remember, men who get money with too great facility cannot usually succeed. You must get the first dollars by hard knocks, and at some sacrifice, in order to appreciate the value of those dollars.

Advertise Your Business

We all depend, more or less, upon the public for our support. We all trade with the public—lawyers, doctors, shoemakers, artists, blacksmiths, showmen, opera stagers, railroad presidents, and college professors. Those who deal with the public must be careful that their goods are valuable; that they are genuine, and will give satisfaction. When you get an article which you know is going to please your customers, and that when they have tried it, they will feel they have got their money's worth, then let the fact be known that you have got it. Be careful to advertise it in some shape or other because it is evident that if a man has ever so good an article for sale, and nobody knows it, it will bring him no return. In a country like this, where nearly everybody reads, and where newspapers are issued and circulated in editions of five thousand to two hundred thousand, it would be very unwise if this channel was not taken advantage of to reach the public in advertising. A newspaper goes into the family, and is read by wife and children, as well as the head of the home; hence hundreds and thousands of people may read your advertisement, while you are attending to your routine business. Many, perhaps, read it while you are asleep. The whole philosophy of life is, first 'sow,' then 'reap.' That is the way the farmer does; he plants his potatoes and corn, and sows his grain, and then goes about something else, and the time comes when he reaps. But he never reaps first and sows afterwards. This principle applies to all kinds of business, and to nothing more eminently than to advertising. If a man has a genuine article, there is no way in which he can reap more advantageously than by 'sowing' to the public in this way. He must, of course, have a really good article, and one which will please his customers; anything spurious will not succeed permanently because the public is wiser than many imagine. Men and women are selfish, and we all prefer purchasing where we can get the most for our money and we try to find out where we can most surely do so.

You may advertise a spurious article, and induce many people to call and buy it once, but they will denounce you as an impostor and swindler, and your business will gradually die out and leave you poor. This is right. Few people can safely depend upon chance custom. You all need to have your customers return and purchase again. A man said to me, 'I have tried advertising and did not succeed; yet I have a good article.'

I replied, 'My friend, there may be exceptions to a general rule. But how do you advertise?'

'I put it in a weekly newspaper three times, and paid a dollar and a half for it.' I replied: 'Sir, advertising is like learning—'a little is a dangerous thing!"

A French writer says that 'The reader of a newspaper does

not see the first mention of an ordinary advertisement; the second insertion he sees, but does not read; the third insertion he reads; the fourth insertion, he looks at the price; the fifth insertion, he speaks of it to his wife; the sixth insertion, he is ready to purchase, and the seventh insertion, he purchases.' Your object in advertising is to make the public understand what you have got to sell, and if you have not the pluck to keep advertising, until you have imparted that information, all the money you have spent is lost. You are like the fellow who told the gentleman if he would give him ten cents it would save him a dollar. 'How can I help you so much with so small a sum?' asked the gentleman in surprise. 'I started out this morning (hiccupped the fellow) with the full determination to get drunk, and I have spent my only dollar to accomplish the object, and it has not quite done it. Ten cents worth more of whiskey would just do it, and in this manner I should save the dollar already expended.'

So a man who advertises at all must keep it up until the public know who and what he is, and what his business is, or else the money invested in advertising is lost.

Some men have a peculiar genius for writing a striking advertisement, one that will arrest the attention of the reader at first sight. This fact, of course, gives the advertiser a great advantage. Sometimes a man makes himself popular by a unique sign or a curious display in his window, recently I observed a swing sign extending over the sidewalk in front of a store, on which was the inscription in plain letters,

Don't Read the Other Side

Of course I did, and so did everybody else, and I learned that the man had made all independence by first attracting the public to his business in that way and then using his customers well afterwards.

Genin, the hatter, bought the first Jenny Lind ticket at auction for two hundred and twenty-five dollars, because he knew it would be a good advertisement for him. 'Who is the bidder?' said the auctioneer, as he knocked down that ticket at Castle Garden. 'Genin, the hatter,' was the response. Here were thousands of people from the Fifth avenue, and from distant cities in the highest stations in life. 'Who is 'Genin,' the hatter?' they exclaimed. They had never heard of him before. The next morning the newspapers and telegraph had circulated the facts from Maine to Texas, and from five to ten millions of people had read that the tickets sold at auction For Jenny Lind's first concert amounted to about twenty thousand dollars, and that a single ticket was sold at two hundred and twenty-five dollars, to 'Genin, the hatter.' Men throughout the country involuntarily took off their hats to see if they had a 'Genin' hat on their heads. At a town in Iowa it was found that in the crowd around the post office, there was one man who had a 'Genin' hat, and he showed it in triumph, although it was worn out and not worth two cents. 'Why,' one man exclaimed, 'you have a real 'Genin' hat; what a lucky fellow you are.' Another man said, 'Hang on to that hat, it will be a valuable heir-loom in your family.' Still another man in the crowd who seemed to envy the possessor of this good fortune, said, 'Come, give us all a chance; put it up at auction!' He did so, and it was sold as a keepsake for nine dollars and fifty cents! What was the consequence to Mr Genin? He sold ten thousand extra hats per annum, the first six years. Nine-tenths of the purchasers bought of him, probably, out of curiosity, and many of them, finding that he gave them an equivalent for their money, became his regular customers. This novel advertisement first struck their attention, and then, as he made a good article, they came again.

Now I don't say that everybody should advertise as Mr Genin did. But I say if a man has got goods for sale, and he don't advertise them in some way, the chances are that someday the sheriff will do it for him. Nor do I say that everybody must advertise in a newspaper, or indeed use 'printers' ink' at all. On the contrary, although that article is indispensable in the majority of cases, yet doctors and clergymen, and sometimes lawyers and some others, can more effectually reach the public in some other manner. But it is obvious, they must be known in some way, else how could they be supported?

Be Polite and Kind
to Your Customers

Politeness and civility are the best capital ever invested in business. Large stores, gilt signs, flaming advertisements, will all prove unavailing if you or your employees treat your patrons abruptly. The truth is, the more kind and liberal a man is, the more generous will be the patronage bestowed upon him. 'Like begets like.' The man who gives the greatest amount of goods of a corresponding quality for the least sum (still reserving for himself a profit) will generally succeed best in the long run. This brings us to the golden rule, 'As ye would that men should do to you, do ye also to them' and they will do better by you than if you always treated them as if you wanted to get the most you could out of them for the least return. Men who drive sharp bargains with their customers, acting as if they never expected to see them again, will not be mistaken. They will never see them again as customers. People don't like to pay and get kicked also.

One of the ushers in my Museum once told me he

intended to whip a man who was in the lecture-room as soon as he came out.

'What for?' I inquired.

'Because he said I was no gentleman,' replied the usher.

'Never mind,' I replied, 'he pays for that, and you will not convince him you are a gentleman by whipping him. I cannot afford to lose a customer. If you whip him, he will never visit the Museum again, and he will induce friends to go with him to other places of amusement instead of this, and thus you see, I should be a serious loser.'

'But he insulted me,' muttered the usher.

'Exactly,' I replied, 'and if he owned the Museum, and you had paid him for the privilege of visiting it, and he had then insulted you, there might be some reason in your resenting it, but in this instance he is the man who pays, while we receive, and you must, therefore, put up with his bad manners.'

My usher laughingly remarked, that this was undoubtedly the true policy; but he added that he should not object to an increase of salary if he was expected to be abused in order to promote my interest.

Be Charitable

Of course men should be charitable, because it is a duty and a pleasure. But even as a matter of policy, if you possess no higher incentive, you will find that the liberal man will command patronage, while the sordid, uncharitable miser will be avoided.

Solomon says: 'There is that scattereth and yet increaseth; and there is that withholdeth more than meet, but it tendeth to poverty.' Of course the only true charity is that which is from the heart.

The best kind of charity is to help those who are willing to help themselves. Promiscuous almsgiving, without inquiring into the worthiness of the applicant, is bad in every sense. But to search out and quietly assist those who are struggling for themselves, is the kind that 'scattereth and yet increaseth.' But don't fall into the idea that some person's practice, of giving a prayer instead of a potato, and a benediction instead of bread, to the hungry. It is easier to make Christians with full stomachs than empty.

Preserve Your Integrity

It is more precious than diamonds or rubies. The old miser said to his sons: Get money; get it honestly if you can, but get money. This advice was not only atrociously wicked, but it was the very essence of stupidity: It was as much as to say, if you find it difficult to obtain money honestly, you can easily get it dishonestly. Get it in that way. Poor fool! Not to know that the most difficult thing in life is to make money dishonestly! Not to know that our prisons are full of men who attempted to follow this advice; not to understand that no man can be dishonest, without soon being found out, and that when his lack of principle is discovered, nearly every avenue to success is closed against him forever.

The public very properly shun all whose integrity is doubted. No matter how polite and pleasant and accommodating a man may be, none of us dare to deal with him if we suspect 'false weights and measures.' Strict honesty, not only lies at the foundation of all success in life (financially), but in every other respect. Uncompromising integrity of character is invaluable. It secures to its possessor a peace and joy which cannot be attained without it—which no amount of money, or houses and lands can purchase. A man who is known to be strictly honest, may be ever so poor, but he has the purses of all the community at his disposal—for all know that if he promises to return what he borrows, he will never disappoint them. As a mere matter of selfishness, therefore, if a man had no higher motive for being honest, all will find that the maxim of Dr Franklin can never fail to be true, that 'honesty is the best policy.'

To get rich, is not always equivalent to being successful. 'There are many rich poor men,' while there are many others, honest and devout men and women, who have never possessed so much money as some rich persons squander in a week, but who are nevertheless really richer and happier than any man can ever be while he is a transgressor of the higher laws of his being.

The inordinate love of money, no doubt, may be and is 'the root of all evil,' but money itself, when properly used, is not only a 'handy thing to have in the house,' but affords the gratification of blessing our race by enabling its possessor to enlarge the scope of human happiness and human influence. The desire for wealth is nearly universal, and none can say it is not laudable, provided the possessor of it accepts its responsibilities, and uses it as a friend to humanity.

The history of money-getting, which is commerce, is a history of civilization, and wherever trade has flourished most, there, too, have art and science produced the noblest fruits. In fact, as a general thing, money-getters are the benefactors of our race. To them, in a great measure, are we indebted for our institutions of learning and of art, our academies, colleges and churches. It is no argument against the desire for, or the possession of wealth, to say that there are sometimes misers who hoard money only for the sake of hoarding and who have no higher aspiration than to grasp everything which comes within their reach. As we have sometimes hypocrites in religion, and demagogues in politics, so there are occasionally misers among money-getters. These, however, are only exceptions to the general rule. But when, in this country, we find such a nuisance and stumbling block as a miser, we remember with gratitude that in America we have no laws of primogeniture, and that in the due course of nature the time will come when the hoarded dust will be scattered for the benefit of mankind. To all men and women, therefore, do I conscientiously say, make money honestly, and not otherwise, for Shakespeare has truly said, 'He that wants money, means, and content, is without three good friends.'

SECTION FOUR

THE SECRET OF WEALTH
by Franklyn Hobbs

'The capitalist is merely a man who does not spend all
that is earned by work!'

Secret no 1

'Money does all things; for it gives and it takes away, it makes honest men and knaves, fools and philosophers; and so on to the end of the chapter.'— L'Estrange

Is Money Wealth? The number of men and women who can now be laying away small fortunes is almost incredible.

At the same time, they can live well, dress well, and surround themselves and their families with all needful comforts and educational advantages.

Money is not wealth.

Earning thousands of dollars brings nothing to anyone— unless it is so spent that 'while one lives one may enjoy more fully the good things of life.' The first of all good things is that one shall have comfort and independence as long as he lives— that means putting money by.

'To maintain prosperity is harder than to acquire it.'

Nowadays it is easy to earn money. Intelligence and business ability come in strongest when a decision is to be made as to how money shall be spent. Shall it be spent in buying rainbows? Or shall it be spent in buying such necessities as will last—and in buying capital?

'A man's capital is what he has left after he has fed and clothed himself, and paid for the ' incidentals' of life which include everything from railroad tickets to a tooth-brush.'

Every day the choice is before every one of us. Here is money. Shall I buy luxury which I fancy or shall I buy more capital?

We cannot do both.

The difference between the rich man and the poor man is the difference in what he buys with his money. The rich man has bought wealth and position. The poor man has bought trash.

A leading financier overthrows another mistaken theory of the man who wants to be rich but has not the gumption to be it:— 'Can't make a million dollars honestly?' he asks. 'Whoever says that is wanting in industry, or courage, or integrity, or aptitude.'

'How is it that some men live in abundance, and have something to spare, while others can scarcely obtain the necessaries of life, and at the same time run into debt?' asks Socrates, the great philosopher.

The reason is,' replied Isomachus, 'because the former occupy themselves with their business, while the latter neglect it.'

'The young man should never hear any language but this:

'You have your own way to make, and it depends upon your own exertions whether you starve or not.'

'To put the whole thing into an epigram:

He who would be poor

'Thinks of life as a goblet to be drained instead of a measure to be filled.'

Secret no 2

'Thrift produced civilisation, and thrift began with civilisation.'

How old is man?

There were human beings on the earth 500,000 years ago, so scientists tell us.

The oldest building on the face of the whole earth is the Sakkarah pyramid in Egypt, built about 6800 years ago.

Think of that! A building that was 2000 years old when Abraham was born!

In a sealed tomb opened in recent years were found the footprints of men who walked there 3800 years ago!

The cave savage began to change into the civilized man who built buildings when the savage learned to keep things, to accumulate food, to store fuel, to lay away skins for clothing, to hoard the shells which passed for money in his day.

Until the human race grasped this idea, people were nothing more than animals, less intelligent than the bees or squirrels who do provide for days in the future.

There was no tomorrow for the savage.

He ate shell-fish found on the shore. He killed animals by throwing stones at them.

He ate what he wanted at the moment, and threw the rest away.

But when the savage began to make stone arrow-heads, he began to keep them, and to give them to his sons when he died. The savage father and mother began to accumulate skins and weapons and to pass them on to their children.

Each generation gave the next one its gains in the way of art, tilling the soil, making boats, or weaving cloth. All that was collected in knowledge or discovery was passed along.

We are inheriting the accumulated knowledge of all the millions who have lived and died and turned to dust during the past thousands and thousands of years! The results of the labour of those who lived before us make the world as we see it today.

Thrift is not a natural instinct in human beings. It is the outcome of bitter experience--not our own, perhaps, but of those who lived and died before us, and who have left scarred upon us the livid brand of Nature's inexorable law:–Those who waste will suffer.

Mankind today retains the results of his labour and thought in two ways-the money he gains he puts into the bank; the ideas and experience he gains he puts into the heads of the youngsters who are growing up.

It is the thrift of individuals which makes a nation strong or weak. 'So that every thrifty person may be regarded as a public benefactor, and every thriftless person as a public enemy.'

'The capitalist is merely a man who does not spend all that is earned by work!'

Secret no 3

Perhaps the most misunderstood word in the English language is the word 'Economy.' Almost everyone will tell you that economy consists of keeping your money instead of spending it. That isn't economy at all because, if you did not spend something for food you would starve to death, if you did not go properly clad you would freeze to death and if you did not provide proper shelter for yourself you would die of exposure or disease. It is surely clear that economy is something besides keeping your money instead of spending it.

Someone has said that the people of America have grown rich through their extravagances, which, in a broad sense, is true. Americans have grown rich because they have spent their money and in the spending they may have appeared extravagant to other people, while as a matter of fact they were frequently not extravagant at all but were spending their own money, spending it wisely and growing richer in the operation.

Penuriousness is a sure road to failure and want; a nation

composed of penurious people is decadent and will soon be no nation at all.

The silly sounding old English proverb 'Penny wise is pound foolish' is not silly but is a very wise saying. Many people spend so much time holding onto a penny that a dollar rolls by the door unseen. How many people we can call to mind who have skimped and slaved all their lives only to die poor.

True economy is the wise handling of not only our money but our things. Taking care of what we have after we have bought it constitutes economy. In many households food is wasted, furniture is abused, clothing is improperly cared for, the house itself is needlessly battered up, the recently decorated walls are marred and soiled, the piano is neglected, the victrola is played with by the children, the kitchen utensils are burned, the dishes are cracked and chipped, clothing not in use hangs on pegs instead of hangers, surplus bedding is dumped in the corner of a closet, garden tools are caked with mud, the new automobile goes unwashed and is allowed to rust—these things are the reverse of economy. They represent the most woeful waste and yet in America they are the rule rather than the exception.

The people of America are wealthier on the average than the people of any other nation, largely because America is a Country of such wonderful and almost inexhaustible natural resources. Half of the Americans would die of starvation in any Asiatic country and in almost any European country. As a people and as individuals, we might be much richer and we can be much richer if we will use more wisdom in the care of the things we have and in the spending of our money. Instead of trying to learn to hate the people who are wealthy, we should try to find out how they became wealthy. Only a handful of the rich people received their wealth through legacies–only another handful made their money through a lucky turn–still another handful acquired their money through great business sagacity, but the rank and file of the rich—and the number of wealthy people in America is enormous. The great majority of these accumulated their money through wise spending and through taking care of the things they possess.

The secret of wealth is buying once for all. When we buy, we should buy a thing which will last; buy something good even though it costs considerably more than a similar article which is perishable. Real economy consists of building a house that will last for generations, buying furniture that will last a lifetime, selecting clothing that is good for more than a fleeting season, choosing carpets that can be used by our children's children and then, having bought these good things, economy demands that we take care of them.

There is a pride of ownership in an article which has been long in the family; you have something which you are pleased to show your friends because you acquired it when a child or it belonged to your grandmother.

If we buy of reliable dealers, if we buy the best they have, if we do not buy at all until we can afford the best, if we take care of everything we buy, if we eliminate waste of both money and goods, we will grow rich and we cannot help it. Money in your pocket is almost spent—money in the bank is a beginning

'Riches amassed in haste will diminish, but those collected little by little will multiply.'–Goethe

'Those who obtain riches by labour, care, and watching,

know their value.'–C Simmons

'Energy will do anything that can be done in this world; and no talents, no circumstances, no opportunities will make a two-legged animal a man without it.'–Goethe

⊂⊃⊂⊃⊂⊃

Secret no 4

'Opportunity, sooner or later, comes to all who work and wish.'–Lord Stanley

Probably the greatest opportunity ever presented to those people who work for the money they get is before them just at this time. The opportunity to work and work properly performed are the chief pleasures of life. No man in factory or field works harder than the baseball player or the football player. No man ever put more muscles into play in driving an ax into a log than are put into action by the golfer when he swings his driver.

Most pleasure is work—real work—and most work can be made a pleasure—real pleasure

The truly industrious man or woman is seldom unhappy for, 'Industry keeps the body healthy, the mind clear, the heart whole, and the purse full.'

Tired muscles produce healthful sleep whether those muscles were made tired with a baseball bat, a golf club, a hammer or a hoe.

The man who does not know how to work does not know how to play and there is no pleasure in life for such a man.

The first thing necessary to happiness and to ultimate independence is for each man to find his proper calling in life. 'When you can do something better than anybody else, you are acquiring power; and if you can do this easily and pleasantly, this is your calling.'

One of the greatest men who died on the Lusitania was fond of quoting, 'Blessed is that man who has found his work.'

Most of us know that we cannot win a place in this world and hold it without performing our fair share of the world's work. Work brings its rewards in the form of good health, happiness, prosperity and a competence for our later years.

The almshouses of the Country are filled with people who thought someone was going to take care of them and insisted that the world owed them a living. Perhaps it did, and they are getting it, but not the kind of a living that you and I want.

The rewards for the worker are greater today than they ever were before and the man who can do more work and produce more than the next man in line is going to win and win big.

Shorter hours and higher pay per hour are both coming to the man who can produce more in an hour. The world's needs must be satisfied—your needs and mine—and every one must produce his limit and urge his fellows to produce their limits to the end that we shall all have more money, more leisure and more happiness.

'The prosperity of any nation is in exact proportion to the quantity of labour which it spends in 11 obtaining and employing means of life.'—John Ruskin

Prosperity for the whole people is the result of confidence of all people in all people.

It was the great Bishop Home who said, 'Prosperity too often has the same effect upon its possessor that a calm at sea has on a Dutch mariner, who frequently, it is said, in these circumstances, ties up the rudder, gets drunk, and goes to sleep.' Present conditions indicate that some people have been playing the part of the Dutch mariner and, drunk with prosperity, have tied up the rudder and gone to sleep, forgetting that there may be others floating about on the sea of life without a rudder who might need assistance.

'To rejoice in the prosperity of another is to partake of it.'—W Austin

'Great works are performed not by strength but by perseverance.'—Johnson

'No gain is so certain as that which proceeds from the economical use of what you have.'—From the Latin

Secret no 5

'The choicest pleasures of life lie within the ring of moderation.'–
Tupper.

The most handsomely dressed man and the most
magnificently gowned woman are garbed within certain limits
of conventionality. The most beautiful house or the handsomest
automobile are never of the really freakish type.

Things of beauty which are also things of utility must
be kept within certain limits in design and colour, if they
are to have that much-to-be-desired individuality, without
being freakish.

Freak notions, wild fancies and ridiculous fads have
been costing the American people hundreds of millions of
dollars annually.

It is not desirable to try to stamp out individuality or the
touches of our own personality in the things we possess but it
is surely desirable to eliminate the freakish and the grotesque.

Lines of simplicity and elegance in our home, in our motor cars, in the apparel we buy and in the ornaments we wear are the things to be desired. They cost less, give us more pleasure while they last and last much longer than the flashy, tinselled folderols, which have been too much affected in the recent past. Simple lines are usually the most graceful; ultra-quality always makes its impression and these two combined add so much to the length of life of anything that they would seem to be worthwhile. By employing a good architect and in planning a simple and substantial home, we can have elegance, convenience, satisfaction, durability and real value at a cost far below the average house with its unnecessary and often unsightly tips and turrets.

In our household furnishings and equipment, if we will give more attention to real utility and simple beauty, we will be able to reduce our expenditures in that direction by a large percentage.

When selecting wearing apparel of any kind, the most careful thought should be given to what we already possess in order that the newly acquired garment shall harmonize and enable us to always appear well-dressed. Some people are able to spend very little money and possess a real wardrobe, while those who are more extravagant dressers, finally find themselves possessed of a mere jumble of clothes and no one garment appears to bear any relation to the others.

These principles may be applied to every part of our daily lives. In the purchase of food for the table, more careful selection will insure a better balanced meal at less cost and such well-balanced rationing will mean better health for the family.

It is not the person who earns the most money but rather the discriminating buyer who apparently lives on the fat of the land, who is always well-dressed and lives in a home which is the envy of his neighbours.

Earning money is an occupation, but spending it wisely is a fine art. There are few people that cannot actually add 50% to their earnings by doing a better job of spending their money.

Economy, Frugality and Thrift are words which are commonly misunderstood. The man is neither penurious nor stingy who exercises his best judgment in the selection of every article he buys. Such a man usually acquires wealth and it is such men and women who have built up the Country.

No one has a right to criticize the man who insists upon quality when he buys and who will not buy until he is sure he is getting his money's worth. This is true economy and 'Economy is in itself a source of great revenue.'—Seneca.

You have probably often noticed that a few people simply seem to grow rich. You do not notice that they are making any unusual amounts of money but they continue to give evidence of having more and more money until at last they are recognized in the neighbourhood as being among the really rich. Such people become rich, as a rule, through wise buying and, after they are rich, they continue to buy carefully and judiciously with the result that they not only remain rich but continue to increase their wealth.

Sometimes we are unreasonable enough to envy the rich, while most of us are unwilling to even try to do what they have done in order to become rich and to remain rich.

Wealthy people usually get their money's worth when they

buy because they have long ago learned the lesson of Thrift. Quite poor people are often extravagant buyers, the well-to-do are sometimes careless buyers but the rich are always thrifty; that is how they became rich and that is how they remain rich.

'The man who will live above his present circumstances is in great danger of living in a little time much beneath them.'–Addison

Secret no 6

'Let all your views in life be directed to a solid, however moderate, independence; without it no man can be happy, nor even honest.'–Junius

He measure of a man's freedom and the measure of his independence depends greatly upon the manner in which he orders his own life.

The only man who is really free and independent is the man who saves. You've looked at him and admired him and wondered how he got along so well.

The man who is free of debt is usually free of worry and therefore free in reality; he is truly free and independent.

Such men are free to work or play, to go or come. They never neglect their work, their play or their families:

Such men do not neglect their health because they know how to conserve physical strength and financial strength. They know how to save useless effort and thus conserve their own energy and earning power and, having earned, they know how to save a proper proportion of those earnings against the time when energy will be less and earnings therefore smaller.

We hear much talk of personal freedom and independence but personal freedom and personal independence are impossible except to the saver.

Each man must earn his own freedom, create his own independence and, having earned them, he knows how to use them and never abuse them.

There is some man in your own town whom you have always admired and about whose evident freedom from worry and care you have always wondered. You know him to be a successful man and you almost envy him. At least you would like to know the secret of his apparent success and happiness. The next time you meet him on the street, stop him and ask him. Such a man is always glad to impart the secret of his success to any worthy person.

And when this man has told you the secret it could be summed up in these words: He knows how to save; he saves physical effort, mental effort, tangible things such as food and clothing and money.

It was some years after the Declaration of Independence before this Country became really free and independent. It may take some of us a few years after the declaration to realize absolute freedom and independence, but those who have the courage to make the declaration will family win and those who have not the courage will be like the seven members of Congress, who did not sign the Declaration of Independence. Most of us do not even know who they were; they have passed into oblivion.

'Men do not have their choice whether they will accept life or not; but they can choose how they will live.'–Emerson

Secret no 7

'Freedom bath a thousand charms to show, that slaves how ever contented never know.'–Cowper

Independence in the full sense of the word means absolute freedom. 'No man is free, who is not master of himself' and no man is master of himself who is a slave to any man or thing.

A man may be 'free, white and twenty-one' and still be an abject slave. He may be a slave to a habit, a slave to fashion or a slave to his job.

Being a slave to a habit, regardless of what sort of a habit it may be, is probably the most abject form of slavery. The free man who directs his own movements is not a slave to any habit.

Slavery to fashion is one of the most disastrous forms of slavery because it not only impoverishes but always leaves unhappiness in its wake.

The man who is a slave to his job is not making the most of his job; if the job rules him, then the job is improperly filled; he is not the man for the place. The man who is boss of his job is the man who fills his position with satisfaction to himself and to his employer; he is, indeed, a free man.

Too many people are slaves to money; they spend their lives working for it and never have any. Other people accumulate money and make it work for them; they are free people.

Freedom and Independence are much misunderstood terms. The most that Freedom and Independence can bring to any one is happiness and contentment.

Money will not buy either happiness or contentment but the mere act of accumulating money and making it work for you creates the proper atmosphere for the development of contentment, which is the highest degree of happiness.

The right kind of a habit to form is the habit of being happy. No one is a slave to this habit, for those who have this habit are the only people who are absolutely free and wholly Independent.

Freedom is sometimes confused with license. 'There are two freedoms: the false, where a man is free to do what he likes; the true, where a man is free to do what he ought.' Every person in the United States has the fullest possible measure of freedom and Independence, which is consistent with the rights of others. Added to this, every person has the opportunity to become personally free and Independent through the accumulation of money and the ultimate development of supreme happiness and contentment.

The only man who is really free is 'The wise man who can command himself.' 'To have freedom, is only to have that which is absolutely necessary to enable us to be what we ought to be, and to possess what we ought to possess.'

Every man has a right, and most men have the opportunity,

to eventually possess enough of this 16 world's goods in the form of money and property to insure freedom and Independence to himself and his family. Beyond this no man need go, given health, to find happiness and contentment, freedom and Independence in the fullest meaning of the words.

'An economist, or a man who can proportion his means and his ambition, or bring the year round with expenditure which expresses his character, without embarrassing one day of his future, is already a master of life, and a freeman.'–Emerson.

'Hard workers are usually honest, industry lifts them above temptation.'–Bovee

Secret no 8

'The art of living easily as to money is to pitch your scale of living one degree below your means.'–Taylor

Taylor lived several hundred years ago when the accumulation of wealth was a slow and laborious process. Were he here today, he would probably say:

'Pitch your scale of living many degrees below your means if you wish to live long enough to acquire wealth and to live easily and be comfortably independent in the later years of your life.'

It is altogether probable that each one of us could get along and be reasonably happy and contented without many of the things which we now have and think necessary. By careful elimination it might be possible to cut down living expenses by 10% or 20% or even 30% and still have everything we need to make our enjoyment of life complete.

Almost everyone has bought something which he never used. Many people own or are paying rent for more house than they can occupy and in this way are making more work, and therefore more expense, for themselves.

Few people pay attention to the buying of things during the season in which they are least expensive. There is a day or a week or a time in every year when each certain thing we use reaches its lowest price Almost all things are seasonable and the season of most liberal supply and least corresponding demand is the time to stock up on that particular thing. The time to buy furs and coal is not when the first blizzard strikes us and the time to buy apples is not in January.

A merchant in a middle western town recently stated that he was selling fully one-half of the furniture in his store at less than it cost to make; at the same time he admitted that he was getting pretty large profits on some certain wicker furniture which was just then in great demand for sun parlours, porches and summer homes. Most people bought their wicker furniture during a period of about two weeks in the spring. They knew they wanted it and could have selected it at any time just as they could now select what they want for next spring and make 25% interest or more on the investment in a few months' time.

Human beings are creatures of habit, and habits once acquired are hard to break, but the person who indulges a desire for some luxury occasionally gets more enjoyment out of it than the one who has that luxury at his elbow every day in the year.

While we are lopping off the things we must get along without, it would be quite easy to lop off a few more things and what a pleasure it would be to discover after a few weeks that we were saving more money than we had ever before thought possible. At least it is worth a try.

It is our belief that after three months' experience in pitching your scale of living below your means, you will wonder why you did not do this before. At least that is one habit, the habit of saving money, which is in no danger of being overworked because, when a dollar is saved, it goes into the bank and immediately back into circulation and every body gets the use of it just as though it was spent but that dollar still belongs to the one who first saved it.

'It is not so hard to earn money as to spend it well.'

'It is far more easy to acquire a fortune like a knave than to expend it like a gentleman.'–Colton

'Wealth consists not in having great possessions, but in having few wants.'–Epicurus

'To acquire wealth is difficult, to preserve it more difficult, but to spend it wisely most difficult of all.'–E P Day

Secret no 9

'A man can get anything he wants providing he wants it hard enough and is willing to pay the price.'

Some men desire wealth and some desire merely peace and comfort and a reasonable degree of financial independence.

Some men desire fame and the applause of the masses while others care merely for the approval of those nearest to them, whether they be employers, relatives or friends.

Some men wish to travel extensively and see the whole world and see all that is in it while others are content to see a few of the most famous or interesting spots and be able to travel just enough to keep in touch with the progress of the Country.

Some men wish and must have for their complete happiness a home in the city, a farm in the country, a summer cottage up north and a winter place in the south while some other man would be equally contented with a modest and comfortable home just far enough away from the heart of town to be reasonably quiet and home-like.

Some men want to be members of many clubs, societies and associations and some other man is happy with his one membership in a golf club or an athletic club or in some one lodge or association where he can meet and mingle with the right sort of men.

Some men desire several motor cars of different types with a man to drive them and another to look after them while some other man is just as happy with one car of modest cost and many men have no desire whatever for an automobile.

Some men must have an extensive wardrobe with different clothes for different days and different parts of the day, while some other man is quite content with his everyday suit and a good Sunday and holiday outfit.

Some men want more and some men want less and each man has a right to satisfy his desires and ambitions, if he can. He has a right to work for what he wants and, if he works hard enough, the chances are pretty good that he will get it.

The man who sets a goal and strives for it is likely to get there; he may be late in arriving but he is reasonably sure to arrive.

The man who sets no mark ahead for which to strive is not likely to get very far. His is a purposeless life and he will never be known for the things he has accomplished.

The man was wise indeed who said: 'Aim high and you will surely hit something; aim low and you will surely hit the ground.'

The man who aims high may not reach his goal but he will get a lot nearer to it than the man who 20 aims low or shoots without aiming at all.

Whenever a man makes up his mind that he is going to

have a certain thing, he is already about half way on the road to getting it, whether it be wealth, fame, position, a home or merely a job.

When a newsboy walked into a bank in a small city in Wisconsin with sixty-five cents and was informed by a teller that he must have a dollar with which to start an account, he turned and left the bank with a hanging head and one or two people who witnessed the incident said a teardrop hit the stone threshold as he passed out of the side door. In less than five minutes he returned to the bank, walked up to the teller's window, doffed his cap and said,' Say, Mister, when I own this bank, a feller can come in here and open an account with whatever he's got and it won't have to be a dollar, neither.'

In that five minutes, the lad had decided to own that bank and the writer had the wonderful privilege of being present at a banquet given to that boy, then 66 years old, when he retired from the presidency of that particular bank in which he has owned the controlling interest for just twenty-five years. It was only fourteen years from the time he dropped the tear, got mad and decided to own the bank until he was holding down an officer's chair in that institution and had a nice little block of its stock in his safe deposit box.

After reading countless maxims regarding opportunity— and again opportunity—we come back to the starting-point and realize that our fortunate turns and conditions have been always of our own making.

Secret no 10

'A smooth sea never made a skillful mariner; neither do uninterrupted prosperity and success qualify men for usefulness and happiness.'–Burton

Prosperity often warps the judgment of the individual and all but destroys discrimination. This is usually made apparent in his method of living and in his purchases.

The tendency, during a period of prosperity, is to buy and to uncomplainingly pay high prices, because high prices are the rule. It seldom occurs to the individual that, by a proper discrimination in the making of purchases and in the ordering of his life, high prices may in many instances be avoided.

In the selection of our needs, whether they be necessities or merely desires, a fine sense of discrimination may be brought into action which will result in a saving of something in every case and of as much as 50% in some cases.

It is a well-known and generally accepted fact that the average American is an unusually good salesman and a remarkably poor buyer. As a people, we have had our salesmanship educated, cultivated and developed to a high degree. There are schools which teach salesmanship and many of the leading business schools have recently been opening departments of salesmanship. It seems that the selling of things receives much attention but the buying of things for our own consumption continues to be done by the majority of people in a loose, haphazard and unscientific manner.

Suppose we resolve to buy only the thing which will best serve our purpose and on every purchase bring to bear the best buying judgment we possess; at the end of the year the result of this careful buying will stand out very clearly.

How many times do we rush into a store and buy something which is not the thing we really wanted and which, when we get it home, hangs in the closet, lies in the drawer or rests on the shelf for months and even years.

Suppose we buy what we need and want when we need and want it and refuse to buy until we get just what we need and just what we want. We will probably discover that a fair percentage of our past purchases have been ill-advised and some of them, at least, wholly unnecessary.

And then there is much pleasure in having just what we want, in having a thing for which we never have to make excuses or offer apologies. This applies with equal force whether the article be a home, an automobile or merely a hat.

There are very few people who do not own a hat, a pair of shoes or some other piece of wearing apparel which they have never worn and which probably they never will wear. It was not what they wanted when they bought it and it never should have been bought at all.

Buying cheaply is not necessarily buying wisely. It may be much better to pay a high price for the thing you want than to pay much less for a makeshift which does not serve the purpose and in 22 the ownership of which you will never be happy.

Paying a high price for a perfectly suitable article may avoid paying a low price for three or four articles which would not last as long and would not serve the purpose as well as the one thing which costs the higher price.

The needful thing is discrimination in buying with the result that, with such discrimination, there will be less buying. The producers will make as much profit, the manufacturers' profits will be as large or larger, the merchants' profits will be even more satisfactory and every one will be happier as a result.

Prosperity may have impaired such little discrimination as we had been accustomed to exercise. Prosperity does not sharpen the wits or develop judgment or discrimination. It is likely to make most of us lose our poise and our perspective. It makes us take more pride in quantity than in quality.

This thought finally brings us to a formula, the application of which to our daily lives may extend our period of prosperity, make us happier and more contented by making it possible for us to enjoy everything we have and to have everything we need or may reasonably want. The formula is: Work faithfully; buy carefully; live honestly; and deal fairly with all men.

Some of these thoughts may sound, in the jazzy glare of today, a little bit old fashioned, but there is nothing old fashioned about having money and the person who follows these precepts is reasonably sure to have more at the end of the year than when the year began.

'it is impossible to live pleasurably without living

prudently; and honourably and justly, without living pleasurably.'–Epicurus

'There are but jew proverbial sayings that are not true, for they are all drawn from experience itself, which is the mother of all sciences.'–Cervantes

ARTICLES ON
MAKING MONEY

◇◆◇◆◇

'The time making money should be greater than the time
that you are spending money.'
-Sophia Amoruso

The Way to Wealth

Benjamin Franklin

Courteous Reader, I have heard that nothing gives an author so great pleasure, as to find his works respectfully quoted by other learned authors. This pleasure I have seldom enjoyed; for tho' I have been, if I may say it without vanity, an eminent author of almanacs annually now a full quarter of a century, my brother authors in the same way, for what reason I know not, have ever been very sparing in their applauses; and no other author has taken the least notice of me, so that did not my writings produce me some solid pudding, the great deficiency of praise would have quite discouraged me.

I concluded at length, that the people were the best judges of my merit; for they buy my works; and besides, in my rambles, where I am not personally known, I have frequently heard one or other of my adages repeated, with, as Poor Richard says, at the end on't; this gave me some satisfaction, as it showed not only that my instructions were regarded, but discovered likewise some respect for my authority; and I own, that to encourage the practice of remembering and repeating those wise sentences, I have sometimes quoted myself with great gravity.

Judge then how much I must have been gratified by an incident I am going to relate to you. I stopped my horse lately where a great number of people were collected at a vendue of merchant goods. The hour of sale not being come, they were conversing on the badness of the times, and one of the company called to a plain clean old man, with white locks, 'Pray, Father Abraham, what think you of the times? Won't these heavy taxes quite ruin the country? How shall we be ever able to pay them? What would you advise us to?' Father Abraham stood up, and replied, 'If you'd have my advice, I'll give it you in short, for a word to the wise is enough, and many words won't fill a bushel, as Poor Richard says.' They joined in desiring him to speak his mind, and gathering round him, he proceeded as follows:

'Friends, says he, and neighbours, the taxes are indeed very heavy, and if those laid on by the government were the only ones we had to pay, we might more easily discharge them; but we have many others, and much more grievous to some of us. We are taxed twice as much by our idleness, three times as much by our pride, and four times as much by our folly, and from these taxes the commissioners cannot ease or deliver us by allowing an abatement. However, let us hearken to good advice, and something may be done for us; God helps them that help themselves, as Poor Richard says, in his almanac of 1733.

It would be thought a hard government that should tax its people one tenth part of their time, to be employed in its service. But idleness taxes many of us much more, if we reckon all that is spent in absolute sloth, or doing of nothing, with that which is spent in idle employments or amusements, that amount to nothing. Sloth, by bringing on diseases, absolutely shortens life. Sloth, like rust, consumes faster than labour wears, while the used key is always bright, as Poor Richard says. But dost thou love life, then do not squander time, for that's the stuff life is made of, as Poor Richard says. How much more than is necessary do we spend in sleep! forgetting that the sleeping fox catches no poultry, and that there will be sleeping enough in the grave, as Poor Richard says.

If time be of all things the most precious, wasting time must be, as Poor Richard says, the greatest prodigality, since, 2 as he elsewhere tells us, lost time is never found again, and what we call time-enough, always proves little enough: let us then be up and be doing, and doing to the purpose; so by diligence shall we do more with less perplexity. Sloth makes all things difficult, but industry all easy, as Poor Richard says; and he that riseth late, must trot all day, and shall scarce overtake his business at night. While laziness travels so slowly, that poverty soon overtakes him, as we read in Poor Richard, who adds, drive thy business, let not that drive thee; and early to bed, and early to rise, makes a man healthy, wealthy and wise.

So what signifies wishing and hoping for better times. We may make these times better if we bestir ourselves. Industry need not wish, as Poor Richard says, and he that lives upon hope will die fasting. There are no gains, without pains, then help hands, for I have no lands, or if I have, they are smartly taxed. And, as Poor Richard likewise observes, he that hath a trade hath an estate, and he that hath a calling hath an office of profit and honour; but then the trade must be worked at, and the calling well followed, or neither the estate, nor the office, will enable us to pay our taxes. If we are industrious we shall never starve; for, as Poor Richard says, at the working man›s house hunger looks in, but dares not enter. Nor will the bailiff nor the constable enter, for industry pays debts, while despair encreaseth them, says Poor Richard.

What though you have found no treasure, nor has any rich relation left you a legacy, diligence is the mother of good luck, as Poor Richard says, and God gives all things to industry. Then plough deep, while sluggards sleep, and you shall have corn to sell and to keep, says Poor Dick. Work while it is called today, for you know not how much you may be hindered tomorrow, which makes Poor Richard say, one today is worth two tomorrows; and farther, have you somewhat to do tomorrow, do it today. If you were a servant, would you not be ashamed that a good master should catch you idle? Are you then your own master, be ashamed to catch yourself idle, as Poor Dick says.

When there is so much to be done for yourself, your family, your country, and your gracious king, be up by peep of day; let not the sun look down and say, inglorious here he lies. Handle your tools without mittens; remember that the cat in gloves catches no mice, as Poor Richard says. ‹Tis true there is much to be done, and perhaps you are weak handed, but stick to it steadily, and you will see great effects, for constant dropping wears away stones, and by diligence and patience the mouse ate in two the cable; and little strokes fell great oaks, as Poor Richard says in his almanac, the year I cannot just now remember.

'Methinks I hear some of you say, must a man afford himself no leisure? I will tell thee, my friend, what Poor Richard says, employ thy time well if thou meanest to gain leisure; and, since thou art not sure of a minute, throw not away an hour. Leisure is time for doing something useful; this leisure the diligent man will obtain, but the lazy man never; so that, as Poor Richard says, a life of leisure and a life of laziness are two things. Do you imagine that sloth will afford you more comfort than labour? No, for as Poor Richard says, trouble springs from idleness, and grievous toil from needless ease. Many without labour would live by their wits only, but they break for want of stock. Whereas industry gives comfort, and plenty, and respect: fly pleasures, and they'll follow you. The diligent spinner has a large shift, and now I have a sheep and a cow, everybody bids me good morrow, all which is well said by Poor Richard.

'But with our industry, we must likewise be steady, settled and careful, and oversee our own affairs with our own eyes, and not trust too much to others; for, as Poor Richard says, 3 I never saw an oft removed tree, Nor yet an oft removed family, that throve so well as those that settled be. And again, three removes is as bad as a fire, and again, keep the shop, and thy shop will keep thee; and again, if you would have your business done, go; if not, send. And again, He that by the plough would thrive, Himself must either hold or drive.

'And again, the eye of a master will do more work than both his hands; and again, want of care does us more damage than want of knowledge; and again, not to oversee workmen is to leave them your purse open. Trusting too much to others' care is the ruin of many; for, as the almanac says, in the affairs of this world men are saved not by faith, but by the want of it; but a man's own care is profitable; for, saith Poor Dick, learning is to the studious, and riches to the careful, as well as power to the bold, and Heaven to the virtuous. And farther, if you would have a faithful servant, and one that you like, serve yourself. And again, he adviseth to circumspection and care, even in the smallest matters, because sometimes a little neglect may breed great mischief; adding, for want of a nail the shoe was lost; for want of a shoe the horse was lost, and for want of a horse the rider was lost, being overtaken and slain by the enemy, all for want of care about a horse-shoe nail.

'So much for industry, my friends, and attention to one's own business; but to these we must add frugality, if we would make our industry more certainly successful. A man may, if he knows not how to save as he gets, keep his nose all his life to the grindstone, and die not worth a groat at last. A fat kitchen makes a lean will, as Poor Richard says; and,

Many estates are spent in the getting, since women for tea forsook spinning and knitting, And men for punch forsook hewing and splitting. If you would be wealthy, says he, in another almanac, think of saving as well as of getting: the Indies have not made Spain rich, because her outgoes are greater than her incomes. Away then with your expensive follies, and you will not have so much cause to complain of hard times, heavy taxes, and chargeable families; for, as Poor Dick says, Women and wine, game and deceit, Make the wealth small, and the wants great.

And farther, what maintains one vice, would bring up two children. You may think perhaps that a little tea, or a little punch now and then, diet a little more costly, clothes a little finer, and a little entertainment now and then, can be no great Matter; but remember what Poor Richard says, many a little makes a mickle, and farther, beware of little expenses; a small leak will sink a great 4 ship, and again, who dainties love, shall beggars prove, and moreover, fools make Feasts, and wise men eat them.

'Here you are all got together at this vendue of fineries and knicknacks. You call them goods, but if you do not take care, they will prove evils to some of you. You expect they will be sold cheap, and perhaps they may for less than they cost; but if you have no occasion for them, they must be dear to you. Remember what Poor Richard says, buy what thou hast no need of, and ere long thou shalt sell thy necessaries. And again, at a great pennyworth pause a while: he means, that perhaps the cheapness is apparent only, and not real; or the bargain, by straining thee in thy business, may do thee more harm than good. For in another place he says, many have been ruined by buying good pennyworths.

Again, Poor Richard says, 'tis foolish to lay our money in a purchase of repentance; and yet this folly is practised every day at vendues, for want of minding the almanac. Wise men, as Poor Dick says, learn by others' harms, fools scarcely by their own, but, felix quem faciunt aliena pericula cautum. Many a one, for the sake of finery on the back, have gone with a hungry belly, and half-starved their families; silks and satins, scarlet and velvets, as Poor Richard says, put out the kitchen fire.

These are not the necessaries of life; they can scarcely be called the conveniencies, and yet only because they look pretty, how many want to have them. The artificial wants of mankind thus become more numerous than the natural; and, as Poor Dick says, for one poor person, there are an hundred indigent. By these, and other extravagancies, the genteel are reduced to poverty, and forced to borrow of those whom they formerly despised, but who through industry and frugality have maintained their standing; in which case it appears plainly, that a ploughman on his legs is higher than a gentleman on his knees, as Poor Richard says.

Perhaps they have had a small estate left them, which they knew not the getting off; they think 'tis day, and will never be night; that a little to be spent out of so much, is not worth minding; (a child and a fool, as Poor Richard says, imagine twenty shillings and twenty years can never be spent) but, always taking out of the meal-tub, and never putting in, soon comes to the bottom; then, as Poor Dick says, when the well's dry, they know the worth of water.

But this they might have known before, if they had taken his advice; if you would know the value of money, go and try to borrow some, for, he that goes a borrowing goes a sorrowing, and indeed so does he that lends to such people, when he goes to get it in again. Poor Dick farther advises, and says, Fond pride of dress, is sure a very curse; E'er fancy you consult, consult your purse.

And again, pride is as loud a beggar as want, and a great deal more saucy. When you have bought one fine thing you must buy ten more, that your appearance maybe all of a piece; but Poor Dick says, 'tis easier to suppress the first desire than to satisfy all that follow it. And 'tis as truly folly for the poor to ape the rich, as for the frog to swell, in order to equal the ox.

Great estates may venture more, but little boats should keep near shore.

'Tis however a folly soon punished; for pride that dines on vanity sups on contempt, as Poor Richard says. And in another place, pride breakfasted with plenty, dined with poverty, and supped with 5 infamy. And after all, of what use is this pride of appearance, for which so much is risked, so much is suffered? It cannot promote health; or ease pain; it makes no increase of merit in the person, it creates envy, it hastens misfortune.

What is a butterfly? At best He's but a caterpillar dressed. The gaudy fop's his picture just, as Poor Richard says.

'But what madness must it be to run in debt for these superfluities! We are offered, by the terms of this vendue, six months' credit; and that perhaps has induced some of us to attend it, because we cannot spare the ready money, and hope now to be fine without it. But, ah, think what you do when you run in debt; you give to another power over your liberty. If you cannot pay at the time, you will be ashamed to see your creditor; you will be in fear when you speak to him, you will make poor pitiful sneaking excuses, and by degrees come to lose you veracity, and sink into base downright lying; for, as Poor Richard says, the second vice is lying, the first is running in debt. And again to the same purpose, lying rides upon debt's back.

Whereas a freeborn Englishman ought not to be ashamed or afraid to see or speak to any man living. But poverty often deprives a man of all spirit and virtue: 'tis hard for an empty bag to stand upright, as Poor Richard truly says. What would you think of that Prince, or that government, who should issue an edict forbidding you to dress like a gentleman or a gentlewoman, on pain of imprisonment or servitude? Would you not say, that you are free, have a right to dress as you please, and that such an edict would be a breach of your privileges, and such a government tyrannical? And yet you are about to put yourself under that tyranny when you run in debt for such dress! Your creditor has authority at his pleasure to deprive you of your liberty, by confining you in gaol for life, or to sell you for a servant, if you should not be able to pay him! When you have got your bargain, you may, perhaps, think little of payment; but creditors, Poor Richard tells us, have better memories than debtors, and in another place says, creditors are a superstitious sect, great observers of set days and times.

The day comes round before you are aware, and the demand is made before you are prepared to satisfy it. Or if you bear your debt in mind, the term which at first seemed so long, will, as it lessens, appear extremely short. Time will seem to have added wings to his heels as well as shoulders. Those have a short Lent, saith Poor Richard, who owe money to be paid at Easter. Then since, as he says, the borrower is a slave to the lender, and the debtor to the creditor, disdain the chain, preserve your freedom; and maintain your independency: be industrious and free; be frugal and free.

At present, perhaps, you may think yourself in thriving circumstances, and that you can bear a little extravagance without injury; but, For age and want, save while you may; No morning sun lasts a whole day, as Poor Richard says. Gain may be temporary and uncertain, but ever while you live, expense is constant and certain; and 'tis easier to build two chimneys than to keep one in fuel, as Poor Richard says. So rather go to bed supperless than rise in debt. 6 Get what you can, and what you get hold; 'Tis the stone that will turn all your lead into gold, as Poor Richard says. And when you have got the philosopher's stone, sure you will no longer complain of bad times, or the difficulty of paying taxes.

This doctrine, my friends, is reason and wisdom; but after all, do not depend too much upon your own industry, and frugality, and prudence, though excellent things, for they may all be blasted without the blessing of heaven; and therefore ask that blessing humbly, and be not uncharitable to those that at present seem to want it, but comfort and help them. Remember Job suffered, and was afterwards prosperous.

'And now to conclude, experience keeps a dear school, but fools will learn in no other, and scarce in that, for it is true, we may give advice, but we cannot give conduct, as Poor Richard says: however, remember this, they that won't be counselled, can't be helped, as Poor Richard says: and farther, that if you will not hear reason, she'll surely rap your knuckles.'

Thus the old gentleman ended his harangue. The people heard it, and approved the doctrine, and immediately practiced the contrary, just as if it had been a common sermon; for the vendue opened, and they began to buy extravagantly, notwithstanding all his cautions, and their own fear of taxes. I found the good man had thoroughly studied my almanacs, and digested all I had dropped on those topics during the course of five-and-twenty years.

The frequent mention he made of me must have tired

anyone else, but my vanity was wonderfully delighted with it, though I was conscious that not a tenth part of the wisdom was my own which he ascribed to me, but rather the gleanings I had made of the sense of all ages and nations. However, I resolved to be the better for the echo of it; and though I had at first determined to buy stuff for a new coat, I went away resolved to wear my old one a little longer. Reader, if thou wilt do the same, thy profit will be as great as mine. I am, as ever, thine to serve thee.

The Man with the Muck Rake

Theodore Roosevelt

Over a century ago Washington laid the corner stone of the Capitol in what was then little more than a tract of wooded wilderness here beside the Potomac. We now find it necessary to provide by great additional buildings for the business of the government.

This growth in the need for the housing of the government is but a proof and example of the way in which the nation has grown and the sphere of action of the national government has grown. We now administer the affairs of a nation in which the extraordinary growth of population has been outstripped by the growth of wealth in complex interests. The material problems that face us today are not such as they were in Washington's time, but the underlying facts of human nature are the same now as they were then. Under altered external form we war with the same tendencies toward evil that were evident in Washington's time, and are helped by the same tendencies for good. It is about some of these that I wish to say a word today.

In Bunyan's 'Pilgrim's Progress' you may recall the description of the Man with the Muck Rake, the man who could look no way but downward, with the muck rake in his hand; who was offered a celestial crown for his muck rake, but who would neither look up nor regard the crown he was offered, but continued to rake to himself the filth of the floor.

In 'Pilgrim's Progress' the Man with the Muck Rake is set forth as the example of him whose vision is fixed on carnal instead of spiritual things. Yet he also typifies the man who in this life consistently refuses to see aught that is lofty, and fixes his eyes with solemn intentness only on that which is vile and debasing.

Now, it is very necessary that we should not flinch from seeing what is vile and debasing. There is filth on the floor, and it must be scraped up with the muck rake; and there are times and places where this service is the most needed of all the services that can be performed. But the man who never does anything else, who never thinks or speaks or writes, save of his feats with the muck rake, speedily becomes, not a help but one of the most potent forces for evil.

There are in the body politic, economic and social, many and grave evils, and there is urgent necessity for the sternest war upon them. There should be relentless exposure of and attack upon every evil man, whether politician or business man, every evil practice, whether in politics, business, or social life. I hail as a benefactor every writer or speaker, every man who, on the platform or in a book, magazine, or newspaper, with merciless severity makes such attack, provided always that he in his turn remembers that the attack is of use only if it is absolutely truthful.

The liar is no whit better than the thief, and if his mendacity takes the form of slander he may be worse than most thieves. It puts a premium upon knavery untruthfully to attack an honest man, or even with hysterical exaggeration to assail a bad man with untruth.

An epidemic of indiscriminate assault upon character does no good, but very great harm. The soul of every scoundrel is gladdened whenever an honest man is assailed, or even when a scoundrel is untruthfully assailed.

Now, it is easy to twist out of shape what I have just said, easy to affect to misunderstand it, and if it is slurred over in repetition not difficult really to misunderstand it. Some persons are sincerely incapable of understanding that to denounce mudslinging does not mean the endorsement of whitewashing; and both the interested individuals who need whitewashing and those others who practice mudslinging like to encourage such confusion of ideas.

One of the chief counts against those who make indiscriminate assault upon men in business or men in public life is that they invite a reaction which is sure to tell powerfully in favour of the unscrupulous scoundrel who really ought to be attacked, who ought to be exposed, who ought, if possible, to be put in the penitentiary. If Aristides is praised overmuch as just, people get tired of hearing it; and over-censure of the unjust finally and from similar reasons results in their favour.

Any excess is almost sure to invite a reaction; and, unfortunately, the reactions instead of taking the form of punishment of those guilty of the excess, is apt to take the form either of punishment of the unoffending or of giving immunity, and even strength, to offenders. The effort to make financial or political profit out of the destruction of character can only result in public calamity. Gross and reckless assaults on character, whether on the stump or in newspaper, magazine, or book, create a morbid and vicious public sentiment, and at the same time act as a profound deterrent to able men of normal sensitiveness and tend to prevent them from entering the public service at any price.

As an instance in point, I may mention that one serious difficulty encountered in getting the right type of men to dig the Panama Canal is the certainty that they will be exposed, both without, and, I am sorry to say, sometimes within, Congress, to utterly reckless assaults on their character and capacity.

At the risk of repetition let me say again that my plea is not for immunity to, but for the most unsparing exposure of, the politician who betrays his trust, of the big business man who makes or spends his fortune in illegitimate or corrupt ways. There should be a resolute effort to hunt every such man out of the position he has disgraced. Expose the crime, and hunt down the criminal; but remember that even in the case of crime, if it is attacked in sensational, lurid, and untruthful fashion, the attack may do more damage to the public mind than the crime itself.

It is because I feel that there should be no rest in the endless war against the forces of evil that I ask the war be conducted with sanity as well as with resolution. The men with the muck rakes are often indispensable to the wellbeing of society; but only if they know when to stop raking the muck, and to look upward to the celestial crown above them, to the crown of worthy endeavour. There are beautiful things above and round about them; and if they gradually grow to feel that the whole world is nothing but muck, their power of usefulness is gone.

If the whole picture is painted black, there remains no hue whereby to single out the rascals for distinction from their fellows. Such painting finally induces a kind of moral colour blindness; and people affected by it come to the conclusion that no man is really black, and no man really white, but they are all gray.

In other words, they neither believe in the truth of the attack, nor in the honesty of the man who is attacked; they grow as suspicious of the accusation as of the offense; it becomes well-nigh hopeless to stir them either to wrath against wrongdoing or to enthusiasm for what is right; and such a mental attitude in the public gives hope to every knave, and is the despair of honest men. To assail the great and admitted evils of our political and industrial life with such crude and sweeping generalizations as to include decent men in the general condemnation means the searing of the public conscience. There results a general attitude either of cynical belief in and indifference to public corruption or else of a distrustful inability to discriminate between the good and the bad. Either attitude is fraught with untold damage to the country as a whole.

The fool who has not sense to discriminate between what is good and what is bad is well-nigh as dangerous as the man who does discriminate and yet chooses the bad. There is nothing more distressing to every good patriot, to every good American, than the hard, scoffing spirit which treats the allegation of dishonesty in a public man as a cause for laughter. Such laughter is worse than the crackling of thorns under a pot, for it denotes not merely the vacant mind, but the heart in which high emotions have been choked before they could grow to fruition. There is any amount of good in the world, and there never was a time when loftier and more disinterested work for the betterment of mankind was being done than now. The forces that tend for evil are great and terrible, but the forces of truth and love and courage and honesty and generosity and sympathy are also stronger than ever before. It is a foolish and timid, no less than a wicked thing, to blink the fact that the forces of evil are strong, but it is even worse to fail to take into account the strength of the forces that tell for good.

Hysterical sensationalism is the poorest weapon where with to fight for lasting righteousness. The men who with stern sobriety and truth assail the many evils of our time, whether in the public press, or in magazines, or in books, are the leaders and allies of all engaged in the work for social and political betterment. But if they give good reason for distrust of what they say, if they chill the ardour of those who demand truth as a primary virtue, they thereby betray the good cause and play into the hands of the very men against whom they are nominally at war.

In his Ecclesiastical Polity that fine old Elizabethan divine, Bishop Hooker, wrote:

He that goeth about to persuade a multitude that they are not so well governed as they ought to be shall never want attentive and favorable hearers, because they know the manifold defects whereunto every kind of regimen is subject, but the secret lets and difficulties, which in public proceedings are innumerable and inevitable, they have not ordinarily the judgment to consider.

This truth should be kept constantly in mind by every free people desiring to preserve the sanity and poise indispensable to the permanent success of self-government. Yet, on the other hand, it is vital not to permit this spirit of sanity and self-command to degenerate into mere mental stagnation. Bad though a state of hysterical excitement is, and evil though the results are which come from the violent oscillations such excitement invariably produces, yet a sodden acquiescence in evil is even worse.

At this moment we are passing through a period of great unrest-social, political, and industrial unrest. It is of the utmost importance for our future that this should prove to be not the unrest of mere rebelliousness against life, of mere dissatisfaction with the inevitable inequality of conditions, but the unrest of a resolute and eager ambition to secure the betterment of the individual and the nation.

So far as this movement of agitation throughout the country takes the form of a fierce discontent with evil, of a determination to punish the authors of evil, whether in industry or politics, the feeling is to be heartily welcomed as a sign of healthy life.

If, on the other hand, it turns into a mere crusade of appetite against appetite, of a contest between the brutal greed of the 'have nots' and the brutal greed of the 'haves,' then it has no significance for good, but only for evil. If it seeks to establish a line of cleavage, not along the line which divides good men from bad, but along that other line, running at right angles thereto, which divides those who are well off from those who are less well off, then it will be fraught with immeasurable harm to the body politic.

We can no more and no less afford to condone evil in the man of capital than evil in the man of no capital. The wealthy man who exults because there is a failure of justice in the effort to bring some trust magnate to account for his misdeeds is as bad as, and no worse than, the so-called labour leader who clamorously strives to excite a foul class feeling on behalf of some other labour leader who is implicated in murder. One attitude is as bad as the other, and no worse; in each case the accused is entitled to exact justice; and in neither case is there need of action by others which can be construed into an expression of sympathy for crime.

It is a prime necessity that if the present unrest is to result in permanent good the emotion shall be translated into action, and that the action shall be marked by honesty, sanity, and self-restraint. There is mighty little good in a mere spasm of reform. The reform that counts is that which comes through steady, continuous growth; violent emotionalism leads to exhaustion.

It is important to this people to grapple with the problems connected with the amassing of enormous fortunes, and the use of those fortunes, both corporate and individual, in business. We should discriminate in the sharpest way between fortunes well won and fortunes ill won; between those gained as an incident to performing great services to the community as a whole and those gained in evil fashion by keeping just within the limits of mere law honesty. Of course, no amount of charity in spending such fortunes in any way compensates for misconduct in making them.

As a matter of personal conviction, and without pretending to discuss the details or formulate the system, I feel that we shall ultimately have to consider the adoption of some such scheme as that of a progressive tax on all fortunes, beyond a certain amount, either given in life or devised or bequeathed upon death to any individual-a tax so framed as to put it out of the power of the owner of one of these enormous fortunes to hand on more than a certain amount to any one individual; the tax of course, to be imposed by the national and not the state government. Such taxation should, of course, be aimed merely at the inheritance or transmission in their entirety of those fortunes swollen beyond all healthy limits. Again, the national government must in some form exercise supervision over corporations engaged in interstate business-and all large corporations engaged in interstate business-whether by license or otherwise, so as to permit us to deal with the far reaching evils of overcapitalization.

This year we are making a beginning in the direction of serious effort to settle some of these economic problems by the railway rate legislation. Such legislation, if so framed, as I am sure it will be, as to secure definite and tangible results, will amount to something of itself; and it will amount to a great deal more in so far as it is taken as a first step in the direction of a policy of superintendence and control over corporate wealth engaged in interstate commerce; this superintendence and control not to be exercised in a spirit of malevolence toward the men who have created the wealth, but with the firm purpose both to do justice to them and to see that they in their turn do justice to the public at large.

The first requisite in the public servants who are to deal in this shape with corporations, whether as legislators or as executives, is honesty. This honesty can be no respecter of persons. There can be no such thing as unilateral honesty. The danger is not really from corrupt corporations; it springs from the corruption itself, whether exercised for or against corporations.

The eighth commandment reads, 'Thou shalt not steal.' It does not read, 'Thou shalt not steal from the rich man.' It does not read, 'Thou shalt not steal from the poor man.' It reads simply and plainly, 'Thou shalt not steal.'

No good whatever will come from that warped and mock morality which denounces the misdeeds of men of wealth and forgets the misdeeds practiced at their expense; which denounces bribery, but blinds itself to blackmail; which foams with rage if a corporation secures favours by improper methods, and merely leers with hideous mirth if the corporation is itself wronged.

The only public servant who can be trusted honestly to protect the rights of the public against the misdeeds of a corporation is that public man who will just as surely protect the corporation itself from wrongful aggression.

If a public man is willing to yield to popular clamour and do wrong to the men of wealth or to rich corporations, it may be set down as certain that if the opportunity comes he will secretly and furtively do wrong to the public in the interest of a corporation.

But in addition to honesty, we need sanity. No honesty will make a public man useful if that man is timid or foolish, if he is a hot-headed zealot or an impracticable visionary. As we strive for reform we find that it is not at all merely the case of a long uphill pull. On the contrary, there is almost as much of breeching work as of collar work. To depend only on traces means that there will soon be a runaway and an upset.

The men of wealth who today are trying to prevent the regulation and control of their business in the interest of the public by the proper government authorities will not succeed, in my judgment, in checking the progress of the movement. But if they did succeed they would find that they had sown the wind and would surely reap the whirlwind, for they would ultimately provoke the violent excesses which accompany a reform coming by convulsion instead of by steady and natural growth.

On the other hand, the wild preachers of unrest and discontent, the wild agitators against the entire existing order, the men who act crookedly, whether because of sinister design or from mere puzzle headedness, the men who preach destruction without proposing any substitute for what they intend to destroy, or who propose a substitute which would be far worse than the existing evils-all these men are the most dangerous opponents of real reform. If they get their way they will lead the people into a deeper pit than any into which they could fall under the present system. If they fail to get their way they will still do incalculable harm by provoking the kind of reaction which in its revolt against the senseless evil of their teaching would enthrone more securely than ever the evils which their misguided followers believe they are attacking.

More important than aught else is the development of the broadest sympathy of man for man. The welfare of the wage worker, the welfare of the tiller of the soil, upon these depend the welfare of the entire country; their good is not to be sought in pulling down others; but their good must be the prime object of all our statesmanship.

Materially we must strive to secure a broader economic opportunity for all men, so that each shall have a better chance to show the stuff of which he is made. Spiritually and ethically we must strive to bring about clean living and right thinking. We appreciate that the things of the body are important; but we appreciate also that the things of the soul are immeasurably more important.

The foundation stone of national life is, and ever must be, the high individual character of the average citizen.

Acknowledgements

This book is a compilation of timeless wisdom on wealth creation and financial success. I am deeply indebted to the brilliant minds whose works have been included in this volume. Their insights continue to inspire and guide countless individuals on their journey to financial prosperity.

The content of this book has been carefully curated from the following sources:

- *Think and Grow Rich* by Napoleon Hill Source: https://apex. oracle.com/pls/apex/lonestar/r/files/static/v13Y/Think-And-Grow-Rich_2011-06.pdf
- *The Art of Money Getting* by P T Barnum Source: https:// www.gutenberg.org/files/8581/8581-h/8581-h.htm
- *The Science of Getting Rich* by Wallace D Wattles Source:https://www.jnfoundation.com/wp-content/ uploads/2022/07/Science-Of-Getting-Rich.pdf
- *The Secret of Wealth* by Franklyn Hobbs Source: https:// www.michelleandanthony.net/wp-content/uploads/2016/07/ secretofwealth.pdf

- *The Way to Wealth* by Benjamin Franklin Source: https://www.gutenberg.org/files/43855/43855-h/43855-h.htm
- *The Man with the Muck-Rake* speech by Theodore Roosevelt Source: https://voicesofdemocracy.umd.edu/theodore-roosevelt-the-man-with-the-muck-rake-speech-text/

I have compiled this book by selecting key chapters and portions from these influential works on money-making and wealth creation.

It's important to note that while the book chapters have been excerpted and may include minor edits for clarity and cohesion, the speeches by Theodore Roosevelt, 'The Man with the Muck-Rake,' and Benjamin Franklin's essay, 'The Way to Wealth,' have been included verbatim to preserve their historical significance and powerful rhetoric.

I hope that this compilation will serve as a valuable resource for those seeking to improve their financial well-being and achieve their dreams of prosperity.

—Abhishek Rana